How to
Get a Good
Reading from
a
PSYCHIC
MEDIUM

GET THE MOST OUT
OF YOUR CONTACT
WITH THE OTHER SIDE

CAROLE LYNNE

WEISERBOOKS

Boston, MA/York Beach, ME

This book is dedicated to Nicholas Wagner.
December 30, 1948–January 23, 2001

༄ཉༀ

Thanks for sitting next to me for so many years in the
Wednesday night mediumship circle. We love you, Nicholas.
Keep watching over us.

First published in 2003 by
Red Wheel/Weiser, LLC
York Beach, ME
With offices at:
368 Congress Street
Boston, MA 02210
www.redwheelweiser.com

Library of Congress Cataloging-in-Publication Data
Lynne, Carole.
    How to get a good reading from a psychic medium / Carole Lynne.
      p. cm.
Includes bibliographical references.
    ISBN 1-57863-291-9 (pbk. : alk. paper)
  1. Mediums. I. Title.
    BF1286 .L96 2003
      133.9'1--dc21

                                        2002153882

Typeset in Minion
Printed in Canada
TCP

10 09 08 07 06 05 04 03
 8 7 6 5 4 3 2 1

TABLE OF CONTENTS

ACKNOWLEDGMENTS

I wish to thank my husband, Marlowe, who sat patiently with me as I wrote this book. He has fixed the printer, helped me find lost files, and encouraged me when I was afraid of missing my writing deadline.

I wish to thank all those who have been my teachers as I have unfolded as a medium: Rev. Irene Harding, Nancy Garber, Robert Brown, Marjorie Kite, Rev. Charles Harding, Rev. Dr. Erle Myers, Brenda Lawrence, Nora Shaw, and Glyn Edwards. It is important to note that, while I am thanking my teachers, I am not necessarily expressing their points of view in this book. As you will find, we agree and disagree all the time. Mediumship is a complex subject, and we debate it constantly.

Thanks to Rev. Rita Berkowitz, Rev. Leo Rogers, Ida Myers, Judy Koeffler, Rev. Susan Ferency, Sondra Adelman, and others who have booked me for demonstrations of mediumship year after year, allowing me to get the experience I needed. Thanks to John Holland for all those referrals, and thanks to Tony Santos for including me in large public demonstrations. Thanks to Bob Olson for putting my name out on *www.BestPsychicMediums.com* and *www.OfSpirit.com*.

Those who have supported me are too numerous to mention. I thank you all from the bottom, the top, and all sides of my heart. All joking aside, becoming a medium and working as a medium is no day at the beach. It is hard work, and many people do not understand the work we do. I wish to thank all the mediums in the Boston area that I work with. We are quite a wonderful community, and I am amazed at the way we support each other year after year. Yes, we hassle each other a bit, but there is great love among us. Actually, we know we have to get along, because if anyone knows that life is eternal, we do. We are stuck with each other forever!

And of course my deepest thanks go to my publishers, Jan Johnson and Michael Kerber, for their belief in my work. It is my hope that with the printing of this book, people who want to communicate with their loved ones in the world of spirit will be able to learn more about the ways mediums work. With this knowledge they will be able to select mediums with confidence and get the readings they need.

CHAPTER ONE

ALLOW ME TO BE YOUR READING COMPANION

This book is for you, for those of you who have lost loved ones to the transition we call "death." This book is for you who want to see if a medium can help you communicate with those in the world of spirit whom you love so deeply. People come to me because I have the ability to communicate with those who have given up their physical bodies and passed on to the spirit side of life. I bring them messages from their loved ones in the spirit world. Some of us call ourselves "mediums," and some of us call ourselves "psychic mediums." We all want to bring healing as we communicate with those who have passed to the other side of life.

My heart breaks sometimes from the look in the eyes of the people who walk into my reading room—the mother who has lost a child, the woman who has lost her husband, the man who has lost his mother. They are nervous as they approach me. How difficult it must be to come and see me, to be so vulnerable. They don't even know me, and they are coming to ask me to connect with a loved one who has passed away. But they are willing to be vulnerable, because they yearn for communication with the spirit of a loved one. If there is the slightest chance that I will bring a message from one whom they miss so deeply, they are willing to come and see me.

Some are not grieving and feeling vulnerable as they walk through my door, but instead are very curious. They wonder if there is such a thing as an afterlife. They come to a reading hoping to find proof that when life is over, the spirit will continue on. Some arrive very skeptical and almost hostile. Their eyes say, "How dare you proclaim that you are in touch with spirits? I am here to prove you wrong."

I pray before I meet each of you that I will be able to communicate with the spirit you want to hear from, but in my heart I know that I have no control over which spirits I will be able to link with on any day. I also know how crucial it is that I never try to please anyone—whether grieving, curious, or skeptical. I need to tell you what I see in the world of spirit, and nothing else. You deserve an honest reading from me, and that is what you are going to get, even if your uncle Sam comes to visit with us when you wished your daughter had come. Out of total respect for you, myself, and the whole world of eternal life, I must give you only what I receive from the world of spirit. You will get an honest reading, and if it is not all that you would wish it to be, I will help you to understand that in time you will receive communication from your loved one.

I am passionate about writing this book for you who grieve, you who are curious, and—yes—you who are skeptical, so that you can better understand the process of spirit communication called mediumship. I would like to offer you information about how to find a good medium and how to get a good reading from a medium. After reading this book you will know some things that will help you choose the medium who is right for you. Some of you, after reading this book, will realize that it is not a medium you need but a psychic, astrologer, or card reader. Or it may be that you do not need a reading at all. Perhaps you need to see a doctor, a therapist, an investment counselor, or even a real estate agent!

If you *do* need to see a medium, I want you to be informed. You may need helpful information, especially if you are grieving. I don't want you to have to fumble around, during this difficult time, as you try to make an appointment with a medium. I want you to know what your choices are.

I OFFER TO BE YOUR COACH

I offer and would like to be your coach as you make a decision to see a medium, call for an appointment, and receive a reading. I want to be there for you before you walk in the door and after you leave. For most of you, I will not be the medium you see, as you who are reading this are all around the world. But I can be in your pocket, in the glove compartment of your car, in your brief case, in your handbag. I can be there for you, and I want you to know I really care about you.

I was not always a medium, or at least I did not know that I was. This spiritual gift was delivered to my soul in midlife, and it was quite a surprise, like receiving a new baby on the doorstep. But I have been a coach most of my working life.

For years I coached singers in New York City, the San Francisco Bay area, and the Boston area. These singers sang in shows, coffeehouses, and in their showers. I have also coached many public speakers. I coached a woman who needed to convince venture capitalists that they should invest money so she could start a business. She got the money. I've coached college professors who were terrible speakers, and they became great speakers. I've coached money managers, who then got more clients. If I do say so myself, I am a very good coach.

And now I am privileged to be able to apply these coaching skills as I teach you how to get a good reading from a medium. I know how to spell things out in easy-to-understand language. I have also given many readings and received many readings from mediums. I know what information you need to be an informed consumer.

I want you to get a good reading, as I know how healing, and sometimes life changing, it can be to connect with the spirits of those who have passed on. While it took me quite a few readings before I had that one great reading that changed my life, it was worth the struggle. When a medium one day gave me a perfect description of my relationship to my mother and father and lots of descriptive information about them—plus my long lost friend, my dog—I realized that we really do survive when our physical body dies. I now know that when I give up my physical body, I will take my consciousness with me as I make my transition to the world of spirit. That realization makes me want to take a look at my consciousness and keep improving myself.

This life-changing experience may not happen the first time you go for a reading. It is something that no one can really explain, and the process can take time. If you want to go on this journey, you have to have patience.

I want to be with you on that journey. I am available to help you. If you are ready, let's go. Allow me to be your coach, and I want you to know that I consider it a real privilege to play that role. Let's get started.

What This Book Is NOT

This is not a book about my life as a medium. While I may tell you bits and pieces of my personal story as a medium, there are many books about famous mediums already on the market. You can read the life stories of James von Prague, John Edwards, Sylvia Browne, and others. I am not a famous medium, and being famous is not my goal. I enjoy traveling to big towns or small towns in the United States, Canada, England, and Scotland, and serving as a medium in Spiritualist churches, spiritual centers, and spiritual book stores. Sometimes I get paid well, and sometimes I work for very little or for free. I am here to serve those in the world of spirit who need to get messages to their loved ones living on earth. But this book is about you, not about me.

This is not a scientific book. I am not going to try to prove to you that mediums really do contact those in the eternal life. There is an excellent book with scientific studies that you can read if you like, *The Afterlife Experiments* by Gary E. Schwartz, Ph.D., and William L. Simon. This is a book that describes many experiments with what they call "superstar mediums."

What This Book IS

This is a book about how to get a good reading from a medium. I am going to teach you:

- To understand what to expect in a reading with a medium
- To understand the difference between the mediumistic reading and the astrological or psychic reading
- Where to find good mediums
- About the different lengths of readings and the fees mediums charge
- What questions to ask before making an appointment with a medium

- How to understand the "evidence" that mediums bring during a reading
- About the way your behavior influences the success of a reading
- About the ways mediums work in demonstrations of mediumship

When you have read this book, you will be very familiar with the ways mediums work. You will know how and where to find a medium. You will also know when you do *not* need to call a medium, because you need another kind of help.

So enjoy this book, and tuck it into your purse, backpack, or briefcase whenever you are on your way to a reading. Allow me to be your Reading Companion.

CHAPTER TWO

THE GREAT AND NOT SO GREAT REASONS TO SEE A MEDIUM

In this chapter, you will learn what to expect from a reading with a medium and what a medium expects from you. You will also learn about the great and the not so great reasons to call a medium.

Not everyone who calls a medium for an appointment really understands what a medium does or what to expect in a reading. Sometimes people call mediums for the right reasons, and sometimes they call mediums when they should be calling for another kind of help. As your coach, my first step will be to make sure you understand the best reasons to see a medium.

Sometimes I get calls from people looking for a reading when what they really need to do is call a doctor to check their health, or a career counselor to explore various avenues of work, or a therapist to work out their emotional problems. I am not a doctor, career counselor, or therapist, and it would not be right for me to try to help people with such problems. I also get calls from people who need an astrologer, a card reader, or a psychic rather than a medium.

Before you call for an appointment, let's make sure you understand what a medium does. In this chapter, allow me to teach you what the purpose of the mediumistic reading is and what it is *not*. Then, in chapter 3, we'll take a look at what the psychic, astrologer, and card reader have to offer. With this knowledge, you will be able to decide what kind of reading will benefit you the most at this time.

Understanding the Terminology Used by Mediums

In order to understand what to expect from a medium, you need to learn the terminology that many mediums use. For instance, I will be using the terms *medium* and *psychic medium* interchangeably, as they mean the same thing. Anyone using either title will be giving a reading whose purpose is to communicate with those who have passed on.

Sometimes talking about people who exist in two different dimensions—the world we live in and the world of spirit—can become downright confusing. To make this discussion simple, let's first get some terminology straight.

When you come to me for a reading, I am called "the medium" or "the reader." You are called "the sitter" or "the readee." Your loved ones from the world of spirit, who will bring me messages to pass on to you, are called "the communicating spirits." If you are attending a demonstration of mediumship, where a medium will be communicating with those in the world of spirit and bringing messages to some members of the group, you may hear the term "recipient of the message" used for the person receiving a message during the demonstration. I will be using these terms as I describe what you should expect from a medium when you receive a reading.

Why do we need all these terms? Because sometimes when we are communicating with those in the world of spirit, it may be unclear who we are talking to or about and whether that person is living or has passed into the world of spirit. For instance, suppose I am giving a demonstration of mediumship, and I am communicating with your aunt Helen, who is in spirit. If her message is about another aunt of yours, Aunt Mary, who is living, then we have to be clear as to which aunt we are talking about. That is why we call the aunt who is in spirit "the communicating spirit." In this case, I might refer to "your aunt Helen, the communicating spirit." Then if I mention your aunt Mary, I may refer to her as "your aunt Mary, still living."

As I describe my work as a medium, I will also be using the term *evidence*. When I use that term, I am referring to the things the medium will tell you about your loved ones in the world of spirit so that you will be able to recognize them. As a medium describes your loved ones who have passed on, she is bringing "evidence" that they are "surviving" in the world of spirit. This evidence is often called "evidence of survival." For instance, if I tell you that I am communicating with Aunt Helen in spirit and that she had brown eyes, wavy gray hair, and a birthmark on her left cheek, I am bringing you evidence that I am indeed in communication with your aunt Helen, who is no longer living in the physical body.

Let's take a closer look at the work of the medium to clarify a few more terms. As a medium, I am able to communicate with the spirits of your loved ones who have passed over into eternal life. You may notice that I am not telling you that a medium speaks to "dead people." From my perspective, people do not "die," but simply shed their physical bodies. The spirit emerges from what has become a useless set of clothes and makes a transition into the world of spirit.

Mediums also use the terms *passing over*, and *crossing over* to describe this change.

The medium acts as a message bearer from those spirits who have come to speak to the living. When giving a reading, the medium sees images of spirits, hears voices of spirits, and senses both the presence of spirits and information about them. Most mediums see, hear, and sense the information mentally. In other words, the medium does not see the spirit sitting there, in the way that she can see you sitting there, but sees images within her mind. We call these "subjective" impressions of spirit. Some mediums actually see the spirit outside of their mind, and we call this type of impression "objective." There are also mediums called "psychic artists," who can draw the pictures of the spirits they see, although these mediums are few and far between.

The medium's job is to receive impressions from the world of spirit and to relate what she receives to you. In other words, if a medium "sees" images of your uncle Harry who has passed on, she will describe what she is seeing, hearing, and sensing within her mind. The medium might say something such as, "I see images of a man and sense that this man is your uncle. He has brown hair and tells me that he passed over with a heart attack. I see an image of the letter *H* and feel that either his first or last name begins with this letter."

What You Should Expect from Me, the Medium

You should expect me to focus all my energy on linking with or communicating with the spirits of those who have passed over. You should expect me to describe those communicating spirits in a way that you can understand so that you can either recognize or not recognize them. It is extremely important that I bring you as much specific evidence as possible so that both you and I can be certain that I am in contact with your loved one in spirit.

If you have recognized or identified the spirit whom I am describing, you should expect me to ask that communicating spirit if there is a message for you and then to relay that message to you. If you do not recognize the spirit whom I am describing, you should expect me to get more evidence. If, after I have given you a lot of evidence, you still do not recognize the spirit, we will have to conclude that you do not remember or did not know the person I am describing, or that somehow I am making a mistake in the way I am bringing the evidence.

You should expect me to be honest at all times and *never* to bring you any information that I do not truly feel I have received from the world of spirit. You should expect me to be true to my work and never to tell you what I think you want to hear, rather than what I am receiving from the communicating spirits.

You should also expect me to be sensitive at all times to the fact that you have deep feelings about the loss of your loved ones. Coming for a reading with me is not some kind of game that we are going to play together. I am going to be in communication with those who have passed into eternal life. These are *your* loved ones I am going to contact, so you deserve to be treated in a sensitive manner.

What I Expect from You, the "Readee"

It is important to know what kind of reading you wish to have and make an appointment for that kind of reading. If you have called to request a mediumistic reading, I expect that you will not ask me to do a tarot card or an astrological reading. I also expect you to be on time and to arrive with an open attitude. I can't do my work if I have to waste my energy trying to cope with a readee who enters my reading room with a negative attitude. That does not mean that I expect you to *believe in* the work that I do. It is not my job to tell you what to believe or to convince you to think the way I do. My job is to bring through the images and evidence that I receive from the world of spirit, *period.* End of story! All I expect is that you be open to the experience and enter the reading room with a friendly attitude that will make us feel comfortable working together.

I am not there to be tested by you (unless this is a scientific experiment), and if you come in to test me, you are wasting your time and your money. If you have made an appointment with me, I expect that you will be open to receiving the messages from the world of spirit that I will bring to you. When the reading is over, how you evaluate what you received is your business, not mine. You may decide that the reading was the best thing that ever happened to you, or you may decide that readings are pure nonsense. Again, I am not there to try to convince you.

Think of it this way: If you went to a store and bought three books, you would not throw the books in the trash as you left the store. You bought books, so you would take the books with you. This does not mean you would have to *like* the books. After reading them, you might decide that they were incredible or that you will never buy another book like them. Your opinions about the books are separate from your original decision to buy them. So, if you make an appointment for a reading, have the reading and be open to the experience. Later on, you can decide what you think of it.

If Possible, Learn about Your Family History Before You Come for a Reading

I will be bringing descriptions of those in your family who are in the world of spirit. I may also bring in people who are not family members but who have been close to you. The more that you know about your loved ones who have passed over, the more you will be able to understand the information that I bring to you during a reading. Most likely you know the names of the immediate family you grew up in, and when those family members who are in the world of spirit communicate, they will be fairly easy for you to recognize. But what about your aunts, uncles, and cousins? Do you know anything about them? Maybe this will be your inspiration to make that family tree with all the names on it.

I Do Not Expect You to Believe

It took me years of giving and receiving readings before I finally believed that I was actually in contact with those in the world of spirit, so how could I expect you to believe it after just one reading?

When I received my first readings, my skeptical side tried to find logical explanations for how the medium got such accurate information about my loved ones. "The medium made a lucky guess!" cried my skeptic within. But another part of me was intrigued and open to the possibility that mediums *were* communicating with my loved ones in spirit. I continued to have readings and began to sit in a circle of mediums to develop my own skills. Over a period of years in which I both received and gave many readings, I became convinced that mediums really can contact those in the world of spirit.

I hope that you can receive quality evidence from mediums so that you can understand and benefit from spirit communication.

But I know that there are many people who will never believe in it no matter how much proof they receive. And that is fine, because we all have the right to our own belief systems, and I intend to respect those who do not come to the same conclusions I have. My husband of forty years does not believe in spirit communication, and we get along just fine! He has had readings and quite frankly is not convinced that mediums have actually been in contact with his loved ones in the world of spirit. While he is incredibly supportive of me as a medium and often drives for hours to take me to my demonstrations of mediumship, he does not attend the demonstrations and does not want me to try to convince him that I am communicating with the spirits of people who have passed over. Some of my friends ask, "How can you handle that?" The fact is, I have had experiences over many years that have convinced me that I am communicating with spirits. My husband has not had those experiences, so why should he come to the same conclusions about life and so-called "death" that I have?

When you come to me for a reading, I will respect your way of thinking, your religious background, and the conclusions that you have come to about life, even if they differ from mine. You have hired me to do a reading, not to try to tell you how to live your life or how to think.

The Great and Not So Great Reasons to Make an Appointment with a Medium

We will begin with an overview and then take a closer look. Before we begin, let me say that these lists of Great Reasons and Not So Great Reasons are broad generalizations, and there are exceptions to many of my suggestions. However, a good place to start is with generalizations. As you become more familiar with mediumistic readings, you can be more adventurous.

Great Reasons to Call a Medium

- You have loved ones in the world of spirit and wish to receive messages from them.
- You question the existence of the afterlife and want to explore this question by having a reading with a medium.
- You have questions about your life and are curious to see if anyone from the world of spirit will bring messages that relate to those questions.
- You have had readings with mediums before, and it has been a worthwhile experience for you.

RECEIVING MESSAGES FROM LOVED ONES IN SPIRIT

The *very best* reason to see a medium is that you want to receive a communication from someone who has passed into eternal life. Only through receiving specific evidence, when a medium gives you descriptions of a loved one in spirit, will you be able to understand that your loved ones have survived the transition that many people call "death."

EXPLORING THE QUESTION OF THE AFTERLIFE

Do you believe that we survive the change called "death"? Do you believe that when you die, your spirit will live on? If you have questions about the afterlife, getting a reading from a medium may be life changing for you. And unfortunately, it may not. If you are fortunate, the first time you have a reading with a medium, you will get such incredible evidence that you will never need proof again that the spirit lives on. If the medium receives communication from a relative whom you knew very well, and is able to bring lots of evidence that you can verify, you will receive the proof of afterlife that you need. For instance, if the medium brings you your aunt Helen and can describe how she looked, her personality, and the way she died, along with a funny story about a day you spent with Aunt Helen at the science museum, you will have good proof that the medium is linking with the spirit of Aunt Helen. On the other hand, if the medium links with a relative you did not know very well, then even if the medium brings lots of evidence, it may be information on events you know nothing about, so that you cannot verify it. In this scenario, you will not receive the proof you need.

When I first began to have readings, I did not know many of my relatives, and while mediums struggled to bring me all kinds of information, I could not say yes or no, as I did not know the relatives well enough. I must say that my lack of knowledge about my family history made it very difficult for me and for the medium. But I continued to have readings because of my incredible interest in spirit communication. I also did my homework and learned more about my relatives. I was then able to understand much more of the evidence I received during readings.

As I mentioned in chapter 1, there was a very special day when a medium told me all about my father and mother and how I related to each of them. The medium's name is Mavis Pitilla, and when I knew her she lived and worked in England. She told me some very specific personal information about my growing up, and then brought me an image of a brown standard poodle that I had raised, which had passed to spirit many years before. How many people have raised a standard poodle, much less a brown one? Brown standard poodles are not that common! The communicators that Mavis brought told me all kinds of things about my life as it was then, and about conflicts that I was having. These were things that Mavis could not possibly have known about me. All the evidence she brought to me was correct, and that reading was worth waiting for. It changed my perspective on life and on the afterlife.

If you have questions about whether or not there is an afterlife, by all means make an appointment with a medium.

Seeking Answers to Your Life's Questions

You may want to have a reading if you have questions about your current life. However, you cannot expect to have a *specific* question answered. It is a mistake to walk into a reading with a medium and say, "I want to know if I should take the job in Oregon or stay here in New Hampshire." First of all, you have given the medium much too much information. An honest medium will not want to know that you are even considering a new job. She will only want to know your name, phone number, and the time of your appointment— *and that's it!*

But let's say you *are* trying to decide whether to take the job in Oregon or stay in New Hampshire. During the reading, the medium brings through images of your father, who is in spirit, and the message from your father is, "I think you should be open to relocation if a new job is offered." You will be impressed, as the medium *did not know* you were considering a new job, much less a new job that will require you to relocate. If you had specifically asked the question of the medium, the medium's own thoughts might have influenced the reading, and you would never have known if the advice that came to you about being open to relocation was from the mind of the medium or really from the spirit of your father.

When I do readings, I ask my clients not to ask specific questions because it will be so much more *evidential* that the answer comes from someone in the world of spirit if I don't know anything about the question. If I know what the question is, I cannot be absolutely certain that my subconscious mind has not played into the reading. I would much rather have your loved one in spirit come through and give you the answer to a question that *you*—the recipient—know, but that I do *not* know. The message that I bring you from the world of spirit has to make sense to *you*, but I, as a medium, do *not* have to understand it.

For example, during a reading, a communicating spirit brought me an image of a plate of lemons. I had no idea what this image meant, but when I described the image to the sitter, she began to weep. While I did not understand who the communicating spirit was or what the image was all about, the sitter knew that this was the spirit of her father and knew the special story about a plate of lemons.

When we finished the reading, she told me why the lemons had so much meaning to her. She and her father had shared information about "natural health remedies." One of their favorite "home-style cures" included the juice from a large number of lemons. Receiving the image of a "plate of lemons" during her reading had special significance for her because she currently was not feeling her best and was trying to decide how to help herself to feel better. When the image of the lemons came through, she was reminded of a remedy that both she and her Dad had used. She felt the image was a suggestion from her father to use the "lemon remedy."

She could have asked me, "Can you contact my father?" But she did not ask me anything. I did not know that her father was in spirit. I also did not know that the sitter was not feeling well and that she and her father had shared information about "natural health remedies." Because I did not have any prior information, the image of a "plate of lemons" was much more meaningful. Without voicing her question to me, the sitter received an answer on how to make herself feel better and evidence that proved her father was in contact with us.

Past Readings Have Been Worthwhile

If you have had good experiences in readings with a medium before, go for it and make another appointment! You are a seasoned readee and know what to expect. *However,* be forewarned that just because your last reading was incredible and meant so much to you, you can't expect the next one to be the same. No two readings are ever exactly alike. Even if you have another reading with the same medium, and she brings through some of the same spirits, the reading will be different. But life in the everyday, physical world is like that, isn't it? If you have a great lunch with your close friend Sally, and you share funny stories and laugh your heads off, the next time the two of you go out will probably not be like the last time. You may still have a good time, but it will be different. Readings are the same. Each time you go to have a reading, the medium will be in a slightly different mood, as will you, *and* so will the spirits who come through with messages. Each reading is a unique experience.

Not So Great Reasons to Call a Medium

- You have lost your wallet and think the medium can tell you where it is.
- You are insistent on reaching one particular person who is in spirit and will not accept messages from anyone else in the world of spirit.
- You want to know if you will meet a new lover.

- You want to know if you should get a new job.
- You want to know if your health is good or poor.

Finding Your Lost Wallet

While I am sorry that you lost your wallet, look under the bed, in the trunk of your car, and around the entrances of your home, but please don't pick up the telephone to call me for help. And if you *do* pick up the phone to find someone who can tell you where your wallet is, call a psychic! *And* make sure it is a psychic who has a good track record for locating lost objects. Now I can hear some of my friends who are mediums yelling as I suggest that a psychic may be a better person to call than a medium to find a wallet. Yes, we all know that mediums have found many lost objects, including wallets. But as I said before, the job of a medium is to bring messages from spirit, and you may or may not get a message about the location of your lost wallet. While it is possible that your uncle Harry in spirit will be able to tell you where your wallet is, he may not. Also, if Uncle Harry has waited all this time to be able to communicate with you through a medium, he may not want to have to use his time trying to find your wallet! He may have things to say about his passing, the family, or about your life. As has been said, when a spirit comes through to a medium, she has no idea as to what the spirit is going to talk about. So if I wanted to find a lost wallet I, would call a psychic experienced in finding lost objects.

The other day, I was talking with my friend Mary Lee, who works as a psychic. She described a fascinating procedure that she uses to help people find lost objects. For instance, if she is trying to find a wallet, she pretends that she is the lost object and then asks herself, "Where am I?" Let's say that she is now a wallet, and she sees herself on the floor. She would then ask herself, "If I am a wallet on the floor, whose house am I in? Which room of the house am I in?" She continues to pretend that she is the lost wallet and asks more and more questions, until she eventually finds out where she is, and therefore where the lost wallet is. Before talking with her, I had never known that psychics use these kinds of techniques. In fact, May Lee used this technique and made a woman very happy by finding her lost diamond ring!

Contacting a Particular Person in Spirit

Don't call a medium if you want to receive a message from the spirit of your mother, and that is the *only* spirit you are willing to hear from. While it is completely understandable that you want very much to hear from the spirit of your mother, there is no guarantee. If you ask a medium specifically to try to reach your mother, the medium will not know if her mind is influencing what she receives. When the medium knows nothing and is not trying to reach anyone in particular, the reading will be much more evidential. If the medium does bring through information about your mother, both you and the medium will be sure that it did not come from the medium's mind.

Don't panic, however, if you accidentally tell the medium that you want to reach your mother. Although the reading will not be as evidential as when the medium knows nothing, it can still be a good reading if the medium works harder to bring through many pieces of evidence about your mother—information that she could not possibly have known beforehand.

The good news is that, most of the time, the loved ones in spirit who communicate *are* the ones you want to receive a communication from. When I give readings, I would say that 95 percent of the time, some of the spirits that my clients want to hear from *do* show up. And most often, when a client desperately wants to hear from a certain spirit, that spirit comes through.

It is very hard for anyone who desperately wants to hear from a certain communicating spirit at a reading, and it does not happen. "Why? Why? Why?" sobs a sitter. "If I really want to hear from my mother in spirit, why doesn't she communicate?" This is a very difficult question, and I refuse to try to give a definite answer. There is absolutely no way I can prove anything about why a spirit communicates on a certain day and not on other days. All I can do is give you my ideas on this matter, and my ideas are only theories.

It is possible that the loved one in spirit is simply not available for communication on a particular day. We do not really know what it is like in the world of spirit, and therefore it is difficult to make judgments about what those in the spirit world are experiencing.

Frankly, I do not feel that I can make concrete statements about the world of spirit, because I cannot prove them. When I bring an image of your relatives, and I can describe their looks, personality, cause of death, and perhaps their names, you, the readee, are there to verify that the information I bring is correct or incorrect. But if I describe what it is like in the world of spirit, there is no one living to verify the information. Forgive me if you find my attitude inappropriate within this world of mediums and readings, but I still need a living person to verify the evidence before I can accept it as true.

Here is another theory about why you may not get a message from a spirit you want to hear from. It is possible that many spirits are communicating during a given reading, and I am only picking up on the "vibrations" of a certain number of spirits. If this is the case, I may not be able to tell which spirits are more important to you than others. In other words, the spirit of your old classmate may somehow be getting my attention, while the spirit of your father is not getting through to me. It may be that the spirit of your old classmate is more assertive and "louder" than the spirit of your father.

Also, even if I see both the spirit of your classmate and the spirit of your father, I may not immediately know how these spirits are related to you. And, as I do not know—and should not know—whom you want to talk to, I am not able to distinguish who is important to you and who is not.

You may ask, "Well, wouldn't it be better, then, if I just *told* you I want to reach my father, so that you could just pay attention to spirits who might be my father?" I would still argue that the answer is no, because when the medium knows whom you are looking for, it is too easy, on a conscious or subconscious level, to let that knowledge play into the reading. Sometimes it is heartbreaking for me to do a reading and not communicate with the person you want me to reach, but if I am to be sure that a reading is completely honest, I cannot have prior information about any of your wishes for the reading. The only exception I will make is this: If I am close to the end of a reading, and the spirit you want to hear from has not communicated, I will then ask if this is a male or female. For the rest of the reading I will only pay attention to males or females, depending on whom you are looking for.

After my mother passed into the world of spirit, it was a couple of years before I received a communication during a reading that I felt was really from the spirit of my mother. I'd had many readings, and many other loved ones in spirit had shown up, but not my mother. I had to understand that I needed to be patient and that eventually I would receive a communication through a medium from my mother. Now you may wonder why, if I am a medium, I need to go *to* a medium to communicate with my mother. I go because, when I think I am communicating with my mother, I always know that my knowledge of her may be supplying the images that come to me. But when I receive recognizable evidence about my mother from a medium who knows nothing whatsoever about her, then I can be sure that I am receiving communication from spirit. I do have to say, however, that at this point in my life I have done so many readings at which readees recognize the spirits I describe that I *know* what it feels like to be in contact with the world of spirit. At this point, I am more likely to believe that when I feel I am in communication with the spirit of my mother, I really am.

When you make an appointment for a reading, *you must be open to whoever from the world of spirit is going to communicate.* I do notice that when sitters relax and accept whoever comes through a reading, sometimes the sitter receives very important and life-changing messages. Sometimes those messages are from loved ones in spirit who were well known to the sitter, and sometimes they are from spirits who were only acquaintances. As a medium, I have come to believe that we do not always get what we want in a reading, but we get what we need. While I cannot verify it (and by now you *know* how important verification is to me), I feel that there is divine intervention during readings, and so we get what is healing. We get what is needed the most.

Meeting a New Lover

There are certain classic reasons that people call mediums. People desperately want to know if they will meet a new lover, get a new job, or inherit a lot of money. First of all, it is questionable whether any kind of reader can accurately answer those kinds of questions, but a medium most certainly is the wrong person to ask. As I've said, the job of the medium is to communicate with those in the world of spirit and bring the messages that the spirits give her. If a communicating spirit happens to talk about a new lover, job, or huge inheritance, then the medium will bring that kind of information. But the medium has no idea, and *should not* have any idea, as to what the communicating spirit is going to "talk about." The communicating spirit may want to talk about his or her life before passing into the world of spirit. Sometimes when the spirits communicate they need to talk about themselves and clear up unfinished business. Sometimes they need to apologize to the readee for something that happened before passing, or say goodbye to someone who did not get to the hospital before the passing. The messages that come through may *not* be about your life.

Please don't call a medium because you want to know if you are going to meet a new lover! Perhaps some mediums will be ready to chop my head off for saying this, as I may be driving away lots of business. But most of the really good and credible mediums I know do not want to be asked questions like this *because we do not know!* Call an astrologer, who will *still* not be able to tell you if and when you will meet a new lover but who can look into the favorable times for new relationships. You may at least get some clues as to when you might expect to meet someone. Or call a fortuneteller who feels she can predict the future.

Personally, as a medium, I do not feel that I can predict the future and have doubts that anyone can do so with any consistency. I have received messages from those in the world of spirit who tell readees what they should expect to happen in the future—and sometimes those things do happen, and sometimes they don't. I once gave a reading to a young woman whose relative in spirit came through and told her that she would be going to South America soon. The readee looked at me as if I had just lost my mind, only to call me several weeks later to say that she had won a trip to South America in a contest at school.

You may wonder why I don't put a lot of credence into predicting the future, when I have experiences such as the one I just described. I believe that the energies are changing all the time, and so if we make predictions about the future, we are reading the energies as they exist at that moment. In other words, we are reading the "potentials" for what can happen. If the energies change an hour later, we might read the situation differently. So while some predictions are absolutely correct and do come true, I don't feel that predictions are correct enough of the time to put much credence into reading the future. I would not have mediums predict my future and live in accordance with those predictions.

I realize that there are many mediums who would totally disagree with me. I invite them to write another book, and perhaps I will learn something I don't know at this time about predicting the future. Perhaps I will become convinced that predicting the future happens enough of the time that I should have more faith in it. Of course, if a communicating spirit comes through during a reading and predicts your future, I will faithfully tell you what the spirit has to say. But it is the prediction of the spirit, not mine. And the spirit may not be any more consistent in predictions of the future than a fortuneteller who is still living in the physical body. So, for me, the jury is still out when it comes to the validity of predicting the future.

I think many readers, and even you and I, can make predictions based on probabilities. For instance, if a man named Sam is an extremely angry person, one could easily predict that one day he will hit someone. Or if Susan is a woman who has changed jobs five times within the past five years, one could predict that she will change jobs next year. But there is nothing psychic or mediumistic about these kinds of predictions. Everyone can make predictions if they look at a person or a situation and use their common sense to predict what will most likely happen in the future.

CHANGING JOBS

Call a career counselor. While I realize it may ultimately be more fun to get a reading than go to a career counselor, do not try to use a reading in a manner in which it is not meant to be used. If you do, you are not being responsible to yourself. That does not mean that in a reading with a medium someone from the world of spirit might not say something to you about your job, but then you have to evaluate what is said in the same manner that you would if the person were still alive. For instance, if your brother Johnny is in spirit and comes through a medium and says, "Sis, I think you should chuck the job you have, grab the old pickup truck, and head out to California," should you follow his instructions? Let me put it to you another way. If your brother Johnny were still alive and sitting in front of you in his dirty blue jeans and torn sweater, drinking one too many beers, and he said the same thing to you, would you do what he said? The truth is that, whether brother Johnny is still living or sending you a message from the world of spirit, if he tells you to give up your job and head out to California, you'd better give that advice some serious thought before following it, unless you are twenty-two and fancy-free with no responsibilities.

If you are considering getting a new job, you might want to talk with a trusted friend, people in your field, or possibly a career counselor. Just because your brother Johnny is in spirit, that does not mean he has all the answers!

Exception: When you have what I call "multiples," then pay close attention. I *do* pay attention to the mysterious power of synchronicity. For instance, if I have a reading, and a medium tells me that my aunt Lucy from the world of spirit says I should be a furniture designer, and I have been thinking about being a furniture designer before the reading, I now have two inputs. If I have a second reading, and the medium brings Aunt Lucy or any other spirit who says the same thing, I now have three inputs. Then if I go to pick up a magazine on my friend's coffee table and it is all about furniture designing, I now have four inputs.

This idea about my designing furniture is coming at me from many directions, and while I do not necessarily decide to become a furniture designer, I pay attention to the messages that are coming to me and carefully consider why I am receiving so many messages about furniture designing.

Finding Out about Your Health

Call the doctor. Again, do not try to use a reading as it was not intended to be used. I consider it totally insane to consult a medium about my health. I go to a doctor. Mediums are not supposed to diagnose your health, and in all the good schools of mediumship students are told over and over, "Do not diagnose. Do not diagnose!" The medical profession gives advice based on years of medical study.

But what if a communicating spirit brings you a message regarding your health? Then you have to evaluate the advice the same way you would if that loved one were still alive. Let's say your aunt Mary, who is in spirit, comes through during a reading with a message for you about your health. You must first ask yourself, "If Aunt Mary were alive, would I follow her advice?" Now, if Aunt Mary was a doctor when she was alive, you might take her advice more seriously than if she was a bookkeeper! But what if the medium, in conveying a message from Aunt Mary about your health, makes a mistake? What if the medium hears a couple of words incorrectly? Personally, I feel that there are too many possibilities for error when a message is from Aunt Mary in spirit, even if she was a doctor while alive. Yes, we have errors in the medical professional as well, but we can go back and talk to doctors who are still living, again and again. If we take our advice from Aunt Mary in spirit, we may not be able to reach her again.

What about Medical Intuitives?

There are people who have the gift of being able to see inside the body, almost as if they have "x-ray eyes." I am fascinated by this talent and have experienced it several times myself. At one point in my life I attended massage school. There were times when I suddenly felt that I could see inside a person's body. I would sense scar tissue within a certain area, even though there was no external scar or anything else that I could see or feel as I massaged the body. I would ask my massage client if she had ever had an injury in the part of the body where I sensed scar tissue, and I was always correct. Frankly, I felt frightened by this ability and prayed that I not be given these images unless I could be truly helpful to people. I did not want to walk around seeing things inside people's bodies and not know what to do with the information.

I have mediumistic friends who are much more talented in this area than I am. They are always concerned about what to do with the information they receive. They know that they should not tell anyone what they see, as they are not doctors and cannot prove that their vision is correct. In fact, many times they are not correct, because while they are seeing something, they do not have the medical knowledge to really understand what they are seeing. A friend of mine who is a doctor told me that she has followed up with some of her patients on messages that they received from psychics and mediums about their health. This doctor said that most of the time the information from the psychic or medium has not been helpful.

On the other hand, I know that some people with this talent are studying in classes for medical intuition, or they are doing testing of this talent. I also know of people with this talent who have medical knowledge as well. I have complete respect for medical intuition, and in fact encourage the study of it, *as long as the psychics and mediums can work hand and hand with the medical community*.

When I meet psychics and mediums who have the talent of medical intuition, I encourage them to either pray that the talent be removed or learn more about it from qualified people who work with both medical intuition *and* the medical community. Personally, I think that there is such a talent as medical intuition and that we will learn more about it in the years to come. Right now, however, it is a new field. I would not consult a medical intuitive about my health, but there may be some of you who are more adventurous than I. If you do see a medical intuitive, please also see a doctor.

Above all, avoid psychics and mediums who "dabble" in medical intuition and try to diagnose your health. You can really become scared to death by a reading that relates to your health, and the reading may be completely wrong. If you feel you must see a medical intuitive, research the field and go to the best person in the country. I myself do not know enough about the field to make referrals at this time.

Exception: There is one exception I will make to the advice I have just given you. If you are feeling sick and you suspect that you have an intestinal problem, *and* a medium who knows nothing about your intestinal discomfort tells you that your sister Lucy in spirit suggests that you see a doctor about your intestines, *then* I would suggest you take it seriously and see the doctor. You now have two inputs. If this happened to me, I would see the doctor. However, if the doctor did not find a problem and suggested that I eat carefully for several weeks, I would believe her. I find that believing medical diagnoses from spirits can be very crazy-making, and I don't care to live that way.

Seeing a medium for the right reason can be a life-changing experience that I highly recommend. I have had many wonderful readings with mediums. Life-changing experiences have also come to me through readings with astrologers and psychics. In the next chapter, I will share those experiences with you. In order to know if it is a medium you need to see, you need to understand the difference between a mediumistic reading and an astrological or psychic reading. As your coach, I want you to be well informed before you make an appointment for a reading with anyone. Then you will know whom you need to see, and why.

A Medium, a Psychic, an Astrologer, or a Tarot Card Reader?

Let's check in and see where we are: You have read chapter 2, and you understand the purpose of a reading with a medium. You also know the great and not so great reasons to see a medium.

Next, as your coach, I am inviting you to look in on several readings I have had with an astrologer, two psychics, and a medium. All of the readings I will share with you focused on me. They taught me a lot about myself, and quite frankly, I had a very good time at each of them. *But they were very different!* By the end of this chapter, you will have experienced that difference, vicariously, and you will be in a better position to decide which kind of reading you need at this time.

If you understand the difference between the readings given by mediums, psychics, astrologers, and tarot card readers *before* making an appointment for a reading, you will be doing yourself and the reader a huge favor! Now, I realize that this may sound obvious, but you have no idea how many times people show up for a reading with a medium and say "Where are your tarot cards?" Or people show up at a reading with a psychic and expect a communication with their aunt Hilda in the world of spirit. It can be extremely upsetting for the readee when that happens, and it is very frustrating for the reader. Just imagine how it would be for your hairdresser if you showed up and asked her to fix your car!

As your coach, I can't think of a better way to teach you the differences between the mediumistic reading and the astrological, tarot, and psychic readings than to let you look in on the readings I've received. But first, let's take a look at the basic differences.

CONSIDER THE FOCUS OF THE READING

If you are looking for communications with your loved ones in the world of spirit, then of course a medium is the right kind of reader to call. If you want the reading to be mostly about *your life*, see a psychic, astrologer, or tarot card reader. As I've said, if the communicating spirits have advice for you, then a mediumistic reading may be about your life, but there is no guarantee that those who communicate will talk about you. When you arrive for a reading with a medium, you and the medium never know what the spirits are going to want to talk about.

The astrological or psychic reading will be focused on your life: past, present, and possible future. The reader will be able to tell you about things that have affected your life in the past and how those very things may be affecting your life in the present. The reader may make suggestions as to what is missing in your life and how you can lead a happier, more productive life. The reader may also have comments about your spiritual life and perhaps your mission in this lifetime.

Readers Use Different Kinds of Tools

While the psychic reading, the astrological reading, or the tarot card reading will all be about *you*, the tools that the readers use to gain information about you during the various types of readings are not the same.

The Astrologer Uses an Astrological Chart

When someone is called an "astrologer," you normally know what kind of reading you are getting. There are very definite requirements for the astrological reading, including the chart that will be created once the astrologer knows the exact date, place, and time of your birth. An astrologer knows about the movements of the planets in your past, present, and future and can create an astrological chart that will describe the planetary influences that have been affecting you from the moment of birth, and that will continue to affect you for the rest of your life.

The Tarot Reader Uses Cards

The tarot card reader uses a different tool to learn about you. She asks you, the readee, to select a given number of cards from a tarot deck, and then explains how the cards that you have chosen suggest information about your life in the past, present, and possible future.

What is interesting about any kind of reading where the readee chooses cards—or throws sticks or coins as one does when using the Chinese oracle called the I Ching—is that the readee is fully participating in the reading. The cards drawn or the sticks thrown will have an influence on what the reader will then relate to the readee. When you participate in such a manner, it is called by some "divination." You "divine" the information by the choices you make as you select the cards, or by the fate that is involved as the sticks, coins, or stones are thrown and then fall into a unique pattern. Some people feel that spirit guides or the Supreme Being plays a part in the choice of cards or the pattern that is created. It is said that there are no accidents in life, and the cards chosen and the patterns created contain great meaning.

Psychic Readers Use Stones, Crystals, and Various Kinds of Cards

I made an appointment at a spiritual bookstore and was told that the reader used tarot cards. Yet when I had the reading, the reader used many kinds of cards, none of which were tarot cards. That was fine with me, and it was a great reading. This woman had started out using tarot cards in her sessions, but over the years had come across several other kinds of cards that she liked using. She had kept her old label, but had moved on to using different cards.

Later in this chapter, I'll describe a reading in which the reader made use of rune stones. If it makes a difference to you what kinds of tools will be used by the reader in your session, ask questions beforehand.

Mediums Sometimes Use Objects As Well

Most mediums that I know do not use any cards or other tools in a mediumistic reading. Many mediums, including myself, do not want to hold a piece of jewelry or other article, either owned by the readee or previously owned by those who are now in the world of spirit. Some of my colleagues disagree, feeling that if the medium can hold Uncle Joe's watch, there is an even greater chance of reaching Uncle Joe. I have a problem with this because if I hold Uncle Joe's watch, I may pick up information about Uncle Joe, but that may not mean that I am in communication with the spirit of Uncle Joe. I may be reading the energy on his watch and getting the information that way. If I want to be sure that I am communicating with Uncle Joe, I do not even want to know that you *have* an uncle Joe and that we are trying to reach him. I feel that if Uncle Joe is meant to communicate within this particular reading, he will make himself known to me.

I also refrain from holding a watch or any article that belongs to the readee during a mediumistic reading, because I want to ensure that I will not pick up any information about my client from the energy that surrounds the watch. During a mediumistic reading, I intend to link with the world of spirit, and anything I learn about the readee should be information that I learn from a communicating spirit, not from a personal article that I am holding.

Now that you understand the basic differences between these types of readers, I invite you to take a look at some of the personal readings I had with them.

My Astrological Reading

I had an astrological reading with Moriah Marston. It turned out to be the best reading of its kind I've ever had. Before making the appointment, I had to do my homework so that I could tell her not only the date and place that I was born, but the exact time. I actually had to get my birth certificate out of the safe deposit box and check the time of my birth. I gave this information to Moriah before our appointment, so she could create my astrological chart ahead of time.

It's All in My Chart

When I arrived to see Moriah, she had my chart sitting in front of her. She was able to tell me all about my quirky personality and sensitive nature—it was all right there in my chart. I always thought I was just accidentally oversensitive, but from an astrologer's point of view, there are no accidents. The position of the planets can explain everything about a person's character. The fact that I have the moon in Cancer in the eighth house contributes to my sensitivity. Moriah could also see that the reason I am talented both psychically and mediumistically is that I have Pluto in the eighth house, and the sun in Scorpio.

My life always takes me in many directions, and you could either call me very interested in everything or say that I put my fingers in too many pies, depending on how you want to look at it. One of my greatest conflicts has always been between time with my family and time spent working. Of course, I realize that many people feel that emotional pull between family and work, but I think that those close to me would agree that I feel that conflict more than the average person does. Guess what? That too is there in my chart. I have the south node in the fourth house and the north node in the tenth house, which represents a karmic pull between family and career.

Moriah has helped me to come to understand what is in my chart, and by doing so, she has helped me to understand and accept my life purpose. I am meant to be a person who will be extremely involved in family life, while also involved in work that is creative and spiritual. It is always going to be my nature to be pulled in many directions, so I'd better get used to it, accept it, and learn how to balance many activities.

Astrology Is a Tool, Not an Excuse!

Moriah does not want her clients to use astrological information in a way that takes away from each person's feeling of personal power.

She does not want them to think that every time there is a planetary movement, they are going to be rewarded or doomed in some way, as if the planetary influences can control their lives. A good astrologist helps her clients to understand that the power is not in the planets but in the individual. The planetary conditions may create various environments that we have to work with, but we can work with whatever the current energies are and still get on with our lives.

Some people like to use astrological information as a great big excuse for doing nothing. For instance, if Mercury is in retrograde—a planetary condition that most astrologers agree causes communication difficulties—it is not an excuse to avoid taking care of our responsibilities. "Mercury is in retrograde, so we might as well forget about doing anything until it's over," some people gleefully declare, as they decide to slough off the rest of the week. This kind of attitude is a total misuse of astrological information. Consulting an astrologer does not relieve us of the duty to direct our own lives.

Of course we all would like to have somebody who could just tell us what to do, knowing that whatever was said would be the right decision and we could all live happily ever after. Many people who go to an astrologer, a psychic, or a medium want and expect the reader to give instructions on exactly what they should do. But responsible readers will *not* do that. As your coach, I would like you to learn to use readings as a tool of empowerment.

Think about how the weather forecaster tells you what the weather is going to be like during the next week. The weather is going to be what it is going to be, and you have no control over it. On a rainy Saturday you can either sit home and sulk or use the day to curl up with a good book and drink English tea. You can decide that even though it is raining, you still want to do the seven errands you had planned, or you can decide to wait until a time when the weather is more favorable to driving around doing errands. It all depends on how much you care about doing the errands, despite the weather conditions.

Planetary influences are not exactly like weather, but a case can be made that there is some similarity. Planetary influences are something that you have no control over. The influences are what they are, and you have to decide how to operate within the existing conditions.

A good astrologer will be able to tell you what lessons there are to be learned from the present planetary conditions. Even though the energies may not be particularly favorable for a new work project, it might be a great time to work off some karma and prove to yourself that even during hard times you can accomplish your goals!

Astrologers Do Not Predict the Future

Please do not visit an astrologer and ask questions such as, "Am I going to meet a new lover?" or "Should I move or look for a new job?" Most good astrologers hate those questions as much as good psychics and mediums do. As I've said, my astrologer, Moriah, does not predict the future, but instead tells her clients about the past, present, and future planetary influences so that they can know what the "astrological weather" is going to be like and plan accordingly. You can take a look at the planetary influences that are operating. You can then think about how you feel about moving at this time, or about looking for a new job. You can think about whether you want to put much energy into trying to find someone to have a relationship with at this time. While the astrologer cannot predict for sure that you will meet someone new, she can tell you about the times ahead that will be more or less favorable for beginning new relationships or finding a new work opportunity.

There is one thing no astrologer cannot predict: our behavior. Moriah does not like to predict the future because she can never know what any client will do in a certain situation. For example, if life is giving me a few rough tumbles, she has no way of knowing if I am going to give up or hang in there. As an astrologer, she can only predict what the planetary conditions are.

Astrological Terminology Can Be Hard to Understand

Moriah has a way of translating what she knows into easy language for me. She has also told me that if there was ever a point in the reading where I felt overwhelmed with the terminology, I should interrupt her and ask her to explain it again, in simpler language. Your astrologer should do the same for you.

My Tarot Card Reading

I recently had a tarot card reading with Mary D'Alba that made me realize I needed to make some changes in my schedule. While gazing at the cards I had drawn, she was able to tell me about my work and see that one very creative piece was missing from my work life. While I realize this comment may seem general, as many of us feel like something is missing from our work life, it was *not* a general comment for me *at that moment.* That day, and for the two days prior to the reading, I had been feeling very sad about the lack of music in my life. I realized I had been devoting all my time to my work as a medium and a writer and ignoring my musical talents. I had been feeling very conflicted and was coming to the conclusion I needed to rework my schedule. (There I am with those conflicts again!) As Mary looked at the cards I had picked and applied her intuitive abilities, she was able to describe the whole conflict to me. There it was, right in the cards!

Okay, I know what you must be thinking! You are right! The conflict was not in the cards, the conflict is within *me*. But I believe that a part of my mind was able to pick the exact cards that I needed in order for Mary to have that important conversation with me. There were literally thousands of topics that might have come up in the reading, but the conversation we had about my conflicts over a creative piece that was missing from my life was the topic that *did* come up that day! The reading with Mary supported me in the feelings I was already having about changing my schedule to include more time for music.

My Psychic Reading

I had a reading with Steven Breen at a spiritual book and gift store called Open Doors in Brighton, Massachusetts. He uses rune stones when he does a reading, and he did ask me if I had a question that I wanted to share so that we could see how the rune stones would speak to the question.

As the reading began, Steven set a lazy Susan on the reading table between us. He closed his eyes and began to settle his mind. As I sat there I imagined that he was calling to the stones to speak to us, and calling on his guides and helpers to bring him information that I would need to hear during the reading. Readers often say a prayer out loud or to themselves as they begin a reading.

Steven began, "This reading will be based partially on what the rune stones tell me. I will receive additional information about the essence of some things in your current situations, tendencies to move in certain directions. There may be specifics that I can work with, depending on how the rune stones lie."

Steven then said, "I would like you to start first and hold this female question stone to your heart. Then take this male stone and hold it close to your throat. And the seed of any question or concern that you may have with you today—let that seed in your heart express to the male question stone any concerns or desires that you might like to come to better terms with today."

I closed my eyes and held the stones to my heart and my throat, and in doing so I began to totally relax and become involved in the reading. As I listened to the flowing sound of Steven's voice, I began to get in touch with myself and experience a part of myself that I often disregard: my inner being. Steven continued: "Hold the stones there for about a minute, and when you are ready, I would like you to put these stones on the lazy Susan anywhere you like, and then spin the lazy Susan three times, gently."

I spun the lazy Susan three times, and the stones moved around and formed a pattern. One of the stones flew off the lazy Susan and landed right in front of me. Then Steven asked me if there was any question or concern that I wanted to share. I told him that I wanted to share a concern about my emotional well-being in terms of working very hard.

Steven asked the stones to express their truth. There was a pause as he tuned in to receive information from the stones and from his guides. Then he looked at the pattern that the stones had made on the lazy Susan and asked me, "Does the state of New Hampshire have any meaning to you? The pattern the stones are making looks like an outline of the state of New Hampshire." I replied that New Hampshire did have meaning to me, and in fact after the reading I would be leaving for New Hampshire for the weekend. He then picked up the stone that had fallen off the lazy Susan in front of me and told me that it was the "stone of confusion." I said that I certainly could relate to that!

Steven said that the pattern of the stones suggested a boundary issue where one might exercise *power over* rather than *working with* certain situations. He continued, "I get a sense of a strong drive to work through issues rather than let them be and let them happen in a more relaxed way. It is almost as if you force certain issues."

As Steven talked about the way I force issues, I could feel my face begin to tighten and my left eyebrow rise slightly. I knew that at any second I could become defensive, but I stopped myself and continued to listen with an open heart.

As the reading proceeded, Steven and I discussed what the pattern of the rune stones implied about my concern with "emotional well-being when I was working very hard." It is true that I often try to control a situation rather than letting it unfold in a more relaxed way. Thinking about the way I operate and being able to talk with Steven in this beautiful reading room with soft, relaxing music playing in the background was an extremely healing experience for me.

Now, I know on an intellectual level that I try to control my life too much, but this knowledge does not mean too much to me because, on an intellectual level, I am able to create an argument against any truth that I do not feel like seeing. I can say to myself, "Yeah, sure you try to control too much, but look at how much you have accomplished. Hey, hey, Carole, if you did not control, you would not have completed so many projects. So don't believe all this garbage about you trying to control your life too much. Controlling is a good thing!" That is my mind speaking—but when you allow your *soul* to speak to you in a reading, it is a different experience.

As Steven let the stones and his guides speak to him, and shared with me what he was receiving, he spoke in soft tones that my soul was able to experience. I had the profound feeling that I *knew* I could live a more relaxed life and still do the projects that I cared about. I understood on a deep level that if I took the time I spend worrying and trying to control, and let my life flow, that time would give me endless opportunities for creativity. In fact, I didn't really *think* these thoughts as I am sharing them with you now. I just had an experience of *knowing*. I have to put it into words now, as I am trying to express to you what happened, but the truth is, the experience was not in words, in my thoughts—it was in another dimension that I cannot give a name to.

When I asked Steven, "What do you call this kind of reading?" he replied, "I have had difficulty for eleven years trying to label what it is that I do. Sometimes it is psychic, sometimes it is intuitive, and sometimes it is clearly divinely inspired. I am not sure that spirit, God—or however you want to define this force from which the information comes—wants me to define it, because that limits it. When I have said that this is intuitive work, the work hasn't flowed. When I've said it is not psychic, it has slowed down on me. When I just trust the universe that it's going to give the information for the person who is sitting there—as *they* need it, not as I want to present it—then the information flows easily." From his answer, I realized that his whole approach to his own life was partially what had affected me during the reading.

What Is a Psychic, Anyway?

Steven's trust in the universe allowed him to accept his abilities without defining or labeling them, but you'll need to be familiar with the labels psychics use in order to request the kind of reading you want. Sometimes those labels can make it confusing to call a psychic for an appointment, because psychics don't always call themselves "psychics." I once called a spiritual bookstore to make an appointment for a psychic reading, and when I got there, the reader pulled out a pack of tarot cards. I said, "Oh, I did not know I was going to have a tarot card reading. I thought I was going to have a psychic reading. Are you a psychic?" The reader told me that she calls herself an "intuitive reader" and that she uses the tarot cards as a tool during the reading. She says that once her client has drawn the cards, she starts by talking about what the cards represent, but then, as she gets intuitive information from her spirit guides, she also tells the client what she is receiving from her guides. I asked her if many psychics felt they were getting their information from spirit guides, and she said that they did.

Logically speaking, this reader could call herself a psychic reader, an intuitive reader, or a tarot card reader, and it would be informationally correct. She is getting psychic information, she is working with her intuition, and she is using tarot cards as a tool during the reading. She also receives information from spirit guides, which to me, as a medium, means that she, as a psychic, also feels that she is communicating with the world of spirit, even though she is not necessarily in contact with the client's loved ones in spirit.

So, as you can see, when a spiritual center or bookstore advertises "Psychic Readings," it is not clear exactly what kind of reading you will get, or how the reader will work. Remember to ask what the reading is called, and if any tools such as cards will be used.

My Mediumistic Reading

Even though I *am* a medium, I also *get* mediumistic readings and had a great reading from Nancy Garber who was named "Best of Boston" twice in *Boston* magazine. Nancy brought me a description of one of my best friends, Pat B., who had passed into the world of spirit. She was able to describe my friend's appearance and her personality. It was so healing for me because before Pat died I went to see her in the hospital in the San Francisco Bay area. I could not stay long because I had to fly back to Boston the next morning. It did not look as if Pat was terminally ill at the time, and so I told her that I would make a special trip back to San Francisco two weeks later to see her. We hugged goodbye and several days later I heard that Pat had passed into the world of spirit. I was devastated. I would not have the chance to take the trip two weeks later to see her. It was too late. When Pat came through to me in the reading with Nancy, it was very healing. I still miss Pat more than I can describe, but at least I know she is doing well in the world of spirit.

Sometimes special messages of hope come in mediumistic readings. Nancy also told me that day that a baby had been born, named Susan. She said that she was hearing from the world of spirit that Susan would develop a breathing problem but that she would outgrow it, and so I should not worry about it too much. I knew exactly what baby Nancy was talking about. Sure enough, this baby did develop a breathing problem and did outgrow it. Susan is now four years old and doing great. Having that message from spirit through Nancy Garber made it easier for me when I heard that Susan was having breathing problems, because I had heard in my reading that she would outgrow the problem.

The Psychic Medium

As you have learned by now, the job of the medium is to bring you evidence from the world of spirit that your loved ones are there and communicating with you. However, there are mediums who call themselves "psychic mediums." There are also readers who do both psychic and mediumistic work. Personally, I do both kinds of work, but never at the same time, and most of my work is as a medium. When I am communicating with the world of spirit, I want to know for sure that it is spirit I am in touch with, and that I am not getting information on a psychic level.

Most readers will be happy to describe their work and will give you a good description. If the reader sounds too confused while trying to talk about the kind of reading she gives, you might want to check in with yourself and see if this feels like the right person to consult. It may be that this reader is what I call a "dabbler" and does not really focus on any one kind of reading.

Beware of the Reader Who Tries to Be Everything to Everyone

In my opinion, the best mediums concentrate on mediumship and do not dabble in astrology. The best tarot card readers do not try to be mediums. Yes, there is sometimes a bit of overlap within types of readings. There *are* psychics who sometimes receive a communication from a loved one in the spirit world and therefore bring some mediumistic work into what is basically a psychic reading. There are also mediums who may get some psychic information and bring that into what is basically a mediumistic reading. But each type of reading has unique goals and purposes. The most qualified reader will focus mainly in one direction.

When I do a mediumistic reading, I concentrate *only* on communicating with those from the world of spirit. I also do what I call an "aura reading," in which I read the energy within the auric field emanating around my client, but this is a different kind of reading, and I do not mix the two. This kind of reading is all about my client and could be considered a psychic reading. However, some of us who do both mediumistic and psychic work are asking ourselves *where* we get the information we call "psychic." Personally, I feel that when I am reading the aura I am still getting the information from a spiritual source. I may not be receiving communication from someone's aunt Mabel in the world of spirit, but it feels as if I am getting the information through my connection to a higher spiritual source. The debate about *where* a reader gets the information she receives during a psychic, aura, or even card reading has been going on for a long time among readers, and I am sure it will continue.

If you are a beginning readee, play it safe. As your coach, I would advise you to get a reading from someone who concentrates on one type of reading. If the reader does do several kinds of readings, please do not ask her to do a little bit of mediumship and a little bit of psychic work. You are not going to a restaurant for a Chinese dinner where you can choose one dish from column A and one from column B. You will be attending a reading, and this is quite frankly serious business. Help the reader to do the best job possible by asking for one kind of reading. I do not feel that you will get the highest quality reading if you ask a reader to do too many things within a given appointment. Some readers may be tempted to do whatever they're asked, in order to please a client; high-quality readers will not let clients dictate to them what they should do.

However, having said that you should never ask a reader to combine skills within a reading, I also have to say that in the world of readings and readers there are always exceptions. There may be an exceptional reader who has developed in a manner that is totally opposite to what I am describing who is nonetheless an excellent reader. Any advice in this book should really be preceded by the words "generally speaking" or "for the most part." The abilities of readers and the kinds of reading available will not always fit the descriptions that you will find in this book.

So you may ask, "Why bother giving all this advice about different kinds of readers and readings?" The answer is that if you are a person who is not experienced at getting readings, it is best for you to consider yourself a "beginning readee." If you are not a seasoned client who can navigate well through a reading that is part mediumistic, part psychic, and with a few cards thrown in at the end of the reading, you are better off keeping it simple and requesting *one* kind of reading at a time. Personally, even though I have had many readings, I prefer to have a reading where the medium focuses totally on mediumship or the psychic focuses totally on psychic information.

Good Questions to Ask

- What kind of reading do you do?
- What do you call yourself? A psychic? A medium?
- Do you use any tools in your readings, such as tarot cards, runes, or crystals?
- What do you consider the main purpose of your work?
- What should I expect to get out of the type of reading you do?

In this chapter, I have shared an astrological reading, a psychic reading with cards, a psychic reading with rune stones, and a reading with a medium. As I'm sure you can see, each reading was a different and unique experience for me. It was fun to share my experiences with you, and I hope you enjoyed reading them. Moriah was a great astrologer and Steven a soulful psychic reader. Mary was very enlightening, and Nancy an extremely evidential medium who brought me communications from the world of spirit that proved to be very healing for me.

Now that you have looked in on my readings, do you know what kind of reading you want? If you want to communicate with your loved ones in the world of spirit, it is very clear that you need to see a medium. As my experience shows, when you need a mediumistic reading, it can be an incredibly healing experience. But as your coach, I want you to know about the different kinds of readings available so that you can make an informed choice.

By understanding the purposes of the different kinds of readings, you will be able to make a decision as to what kind of reading you need before picking up the telephone to make an appointment. You will not call a medium when you want a psychic, you will not call a psychic when you want an astrologer, and you will not call a reader of any kind when you really need a therapist, career counselor, or financial advisor. So for heaven's sake, if you want to buy a new house, see a real estate agent. And if you need a doctor, call one!

CHAPTER FOUR

WHERE TO FIND A GOOD MEDIUM

Where are we in the process? In chapter 2 you learned what to expect in a reading from a medium. Then in chapter 3 you learned the differences between a reading with a medium and a reading with an astrologer, psychic, or card reader. You have all the information you need to decide if you want a reading with a medium. Next, you need to learn where to find a good medium. First I'll tell you what your options are, and then give you my opinion on the pros and cons of the various options. I'll also give you a few tips on where to find a good psychic or astrologer. Then, like any good coach, I have to tell you to make up your own mind.

WARNING: DO NOT TELL THE MEDIUM ANYTHING

Write yourself a note that says *Remember not to tell the medium anything about yourself when you ask for an appointment!* It is a natural inclination to give anyone details when we are asking for a service. When you call the dentist, you tell the secretary not only your name, but also that you want to have a tooth filled or that you need a yearly checkup. When you call to make an appointment to have your car serviced, you tell the mechanic if you want new tires or if you need the brakes checked. But when you talk with a medium about making an appointment, the medium does not want to know anything about you, so you have to fight what is a normal inclination to talk about yourself. Just ask questions about the reading, and give your name and phone number only. Of course the medium will want to know that you hope to hear from loved ones in spirit, but she will not want to know *whom* you want to hear from.

YOU HAVE OPTIONS!

You have decided that you want to have a reading from a medium. Now you need to compare the various options available to you. Honestly, there is no best place to find a medium. Ultimately it comes down to the individual medium, the evidence the medium can bring, and how you react to that reader. However, I can make general statements about the various places to find mediums and the upsides and downsides of the various options. If you are in grief, you may want to consider different options than if you are just curious. If you have had many readings, you may want to consider different options than if you are having a reading with a medium for the first time.

Here are some of your options:

- The religion of Spiritualism
- New Age bookstores
- Spiritual centers
- Well-publicized and terribly famous mediums
- Phone readings and 1-800 numbers
- Internet Web sites

The Religion of Spiritualism

"Spiritualism" is a religion that was founded in the United States in the mid-nineteenth century. Although many people today do not know about it, Spiritualist churches are located all over the United States, Great Britain, and many other countries (see Resources for lists of Spiritualist organizations).

A Spiritualist church service is conducted like worship services in many other religions in that hymns are often sung, prayers are read, there is a period of hands-on spiritual healing, and a lecture is given. While the religion of Spiritualism has no dogma or creed, Spiritualists do believe in a supreme power, which is often called "The Infinite Spirit," and they have a set of principles to live by, one of which is the Golden Rule. There is also a principle of "Personal Responsibility," which states that each one of us is responsible for our own happiness or unhappiness.

Like many other religions, Spiritualism embraces the belief that there is an afterlife and that the spirit survives the change called death and continues on to live in an eternal dimension. However, Spiritualists know and demonstrate that they can communicate with those who have passed over. The main difference between the Spiritualist church service and other religions services is that there is a period of time in which a demonstration of mediumship is given. In fact, some mediums feel that spirit communication is so sacred that communicating with spirit should only be done within a Spiritualist church or organization. They see mediumship as a sacred part of the religion of Spiritualism.

Other mediums do not see spirit communication as part of a religion, but as a spiritual gift that can be shared with others within many different settings. These mediums tend to work in spiritual centers, in spiritual bookstores—both of which are discussed below—or in their own offices.

Some mediums believe that spirit communication can be properly shared both within the religion of Spiritualism and within other settings. I am part of this group. I am a certified medium and minister with the American Federation of Spiritualist Churches. While I work within A.F.S.C. churches, I also serve many churches under the organization called The National Spiritualist Association of Churches, as well as churches that are independent of a larger umbrella organization. My own belief is that spirit communication needs to be shared both inside and outside of the Spiritualist church, as some people are interested in going to church and some are not. However, I do feel that the religion of Spiritualism, for the most part, does a superior job of stressing the importance of the sacred aspect of spirit communication.

The Mediumship Demonstration

In a Spiritualist service, a medium stands before the congregation and communicates with loved ones in the world of spirit, bringing messages to those sitting in the congregation. Not everyone in the congregation will receive a message; however, many are touched by the demonstration. There is no fee for the service, but a collection plate is passed during the service, as is customary in most churches. If anyone would like to have a private reading, she can speak with the medium about it after the service. The medium will normally charge a fee for the reading.

There are a small number of Spiritualist mediums who do not charge a fee, as they feel that spiritual work should not require a payment. Spiritualist ministers who give readings may or may not accept payment. Sometimes when a readee asks what the fee is, the minister will request a donation to the church instead of payment. But you should expect to pay a fee or make a donation, as mediums, ministers, and the churches have bills to pay like the rest of us.

Most Spiritualist churches and organizations also have days called "mediums' days" or "spiritual days." On these days, Spiritualist mediums are available to give short readings to individuals. A very nominal fee is normally charged, and in most cases it is donated to the church to help pay the rent, mortgage, or other expenses involved in keeping the doors of the church open.

FINDING A MEDIUM

One of the best ways to find a medium is to attend a demonstration of mediumship in a Spiritualist church. Not only will this give you an opportunity to learn what spirit communication is all about but if you like the medium who gives the demonstration, you can ask her, after the service, if she does private readings.

If you choose to see a medium who is connected to a Spiritualist church, you should expect someone who has received formal training in mediumship. Many Spiritualist organizations offer courses in mediumship, and students complete both written exams and test church services, where their abilities as a medium are evaluated. Students who pass these exams are certified by the Spiritualist organization that they belong to. Spiritualist organizations around the world train people who know they have the gift of mediumship, as well as those who discover their gifts within the Spiritualist circle. Some churches also offer free readings by students who they feel are ready to do practice readings.

Calling a medium affiliated with, and certified by, a Spiritualist church or organization is one of your options if you want a reading with a medium. You can also call a Spiritualist church or organization and ask for a referral.

Another advantage of finding a medium through a Spiritualist church is that you are receiving your reading within a spiritual community that may be able to help you in other ways as you cope with the loss of a loved one. A Spiritualist minister can offer you compassionate understanding during your sadness and grief and may be able to refer you to a therapist or other professional who could also be helpful. And if you attend the church regularly, you may become friends with others who are also experiencing the loss of a loved one.

Although attending a Spiritualist church service may be an excellent option for you, if you are grieving for a loved one, it is important for you to know that not everyone in the congregation will receive a reading at the service. Even if you do get a reading during the service, it will be a short message, as the medium must get to others besides you during the demonstration. If you are impressed by the medium who gives a demonstration of mediumship during the service, ask that medium for a private appointment at a later date. You can also get referrals from the pastor of the church or other people whom you meet at a Spiritualist church. You do not have to be a Spiritualist, or ever intend to become one, in order to attend a service and receive a private reading with a Spiritualist medium at a later date.

The New Age Bookstore

There are many bookstores around the United States, and in many other countries, that call themselves "New Age bookstores" or "spiritual bookstores." Some use the term "occult bookstore." The readers associated with these bookstores usually do psychic, astrological, and card readings, but more and more New Age bookstores are offering mediumistic readings as well. These establishments sell books on many spiritual and self-help topics, as well as tarot cards, crystal balls, jewelry, and many other gift items. Readers usually have a place to sit at the back of the store, where there are small tables with two chairs: one for the reader and one for the readee. Sometimes an appointment is necessary, but more often than not "walk-ins" are encouraged. A fee will be charged for readings, and that fee will be divided between the bookstore and the medium.

The Spiritual Center

There are many spiritual centers—also called colleges, schools, institutes, federations or associations—that offer all kinds of workshops and seminars on spirituality and self-help. They often have correspondence courses as well as residential weekend or seven-day courses. Most offer demonstrations of mediumship and readings. Some examples in the United States are The American Federation of Spiritualist Churches and the National Spiritualist Association of Churches. The Rowe Camp and Conference Center in Rowe Massachusetts rents space to workshop leaders and sponsors many of their own programs. Some examples in Europe are the Arthur Findlay College in Stansted, England; the Edinburgh College of Parapsychology in Scotland; and the International Spiritualist Federation, which holds each conference in a different part of the world. Contact information can be found in the Resources section at the end of this book. You can also find the names of many centers and schools that offer both classes and mediumistic readings in both national and local New Age magazines.

You may need to make an appointment for a reading at a center, as the medium may also be giving workshops and have only limited time available for readings. A fee will be charged for readings. Most likely the fee will be divided between the medium and the center, unless the medium has paid a rental fee for use of the reading room.

Atmosphere

I cannot give you my opinions about where to find the best mediums without revealing to you that I do not like spooky places. I suggest that whenever you call to make an appointment for any kind of reading ask, "Where do you give your readings? What is the atmosphere like?"

Personally, if I am getting a private reading I prefer to go to a Spiritualist church, a lovely bookstore, or the reading room of a medium, which is often in her home. If you are getting a reading, you may wish to know what kind of atmosphere you will be experiencing.

I know people who are intrigued by ghostlike images and dimly lit rooms, and I know other people who would never want to get a reading outside of a Spiritualist church. There are all kinds of places to receive readings, and the place may affect you. There are bookstores that offer readings in an extremely mysterious atmosphere, which appeals to some people. There are bookstores that have a more angelic atmosphere. It is really hard to categorize these places, but if you are going to get a reading in a spiritual bookstore or center, you may want to make a visit to the location to see if you feel comfortable with the "vibes" of the place.

As I said, I don't like spooky places. But some of my friends *love* haunted houses and ghost towns. They would enjoy receiving readings in places that I can't sit in without feeling uncomfortable. I just don't like chills running up and down my spine. I would rather be in a Spiritualist church or a bookstore or center where the energy feels very spiritual and not at all spooky.

By the way, I am grateful that there *are* mediums who like to visit haunted houses and who can bust the ghosts that need busting. There are some spirits out there that cause trouble, and I am glad that some other mediums can cope with those spooky spirits so that if you have a mischievous ghost in your house you can call *them* instead of me!

If you like the vibrations of the spooky and mysterious, go with my friends and I will stay home with a good book and listen to music. The main point is, *you* have to be comfortable with the place where you will receive a reading.

One Caution

If you are in grief, before looking for a medium in a bookstore or a spiritual center, get a recommendation from a friend, rather than have a reading with a complete stranger. This is not a good time for you to experiment. The readers who work in these locations may or may not give public demonstrations, and so you may not be able to watch them work before asking for a private appointment. Remember, when you do meet a medium with whom you would like to have a reading, that medium will be attempting to communicate with your loved ones in the world of spirit. You need a medium who respects the sanctity of spirit communication and will treat you with respect and dignity.

Well-Publicized and Terribly Famous Mediums

There are a number of mediums who give demonstrations of spirit communication on television and radio. Many of these more public mediums have books on the market that you can buy at your local New Age or mainstream bookstore. If the medium appears on television or radio, or gives demonstrations of mediumship in a hotel ballroom or other meeting hall, there is often a phone number to call. If the medium has published a book, information on how to contact the medium is printed in the book.

Some mediums are now advertising their services on radio and television and in New Age and alternative health magazines. As with any other advertised service, contact information is always available.

Attending a Large Demonstration in a Hotel or Concert Hall

If, while you are in grief, you decide to go to a demonstration of mediumship given by a well-known medium in a hotel or concert hall, make sure that you know *and accept* the fact that most likely you will not receive a message from your loved ones in spirit during this demonstration. In a large demonstration, the odds are very much against it, as these demonstrations often seat more than three hundred people. The purpose of these large demonstrations is to give many people an opportunity to watch a medium, or a number of different mediums, work. If you see a medium work and want to have a private reading with the medium, contact information is always available at the demonstration. While promoters of such demonstrations never guarantee that everyone will receive a reading, many people still arrive with great expectations that they will get a message.

I occasionally work in these large demonstrations, and they are often wonderful, lively events because so many people are sharing the experience together. However, when I talk to people in the lobby after the demonstration, some are very upset that they did not receive readings. I hear the same complaints from those who attend church services and expect to get a reading. Anyone who attends a demonstration, large or small, in a concert hall or a church, must understand that this is a *demonstration*, not a format where everyone gets a message.

Some who have not received readings tell me that they have prayed to their relatives in the world of spirit before the demonstration, and then have felt let down when their loved ones in spirit did not come through in the demonstration. One woman told me, "I prayed to my husband in spirit to get through to the medium so that I would get a message. What is wrong with my husband? Did he not come to this demonstration, or if he did, why didn't he get through to the medium?"

I told this woman that spirit communication simply does not work that way. One cannot pray to a particular spirit and then go to a demonstration of mediumship, or even to a private reading, and expect that particular spirit to communicate. As I have said earlier in this book, a medium does not know which communicating spirits will come through in a private reading, much less in a demonstration. In a large demonstration, the odds are very much against getting a message.

When people are having deep feelings of grief and are upset that they have not received a reading in a large demonstration, they are in no mood to hear about the numbers of people and the odds of getting a reading. If you are in grief, I encourage you to find a way to have a private reading with a medium and stay away from demonstrations, unless you are able to handle the fact that this is a way to *learn* about mediumship, and not a format in which you are likely to receive a message from your loved one.

The other side of the coin is that some people in grief who attend large demonstrations are really cheered up by the experience. Even though they may not get a message, they are encouraged by seeing others receive messages. As they listen to each message being given, they know that they too will be able to receive a communication from a loved one at a later date by making an appointment for a private reading or by attending a message circle, in which everyone will receive a reading.

Some people prefer the fun and often humorous atmosphere of the large demonstration in a concert hall or hotel ballroom. While the demonstration of mediumship in a Spiritualist church has a more sacred feeling, and the environment is often peaceful and quiet, the atmosphere in the large demonstration is often filled with laughter and applause, and sometimes emotional testimonies are given by those in the audience. This is not to say that you will not hear some laughter in the Spiritualist church service. However, I have found a church service to have a totally different atmosphere from that of a large demonstration.

I am personally comfortable with demonstrations in churches and with large demonstrations that are not offered in a religious context, and I feel that I benefit from both. But as your coach, I have to be honest with you and tell you that many people are only comfortable in one setting or the other. So if you are in grief, ask yourself which setting you will find more comfortable when attending a demonstration.

The Incredibly Famous Mediums

These days there are some very famous mediums. Some of them are highly talented—and some are just very famous. Being well known does not make someone a great medium or the right medium for you.

Some mediums are famous because they are incredibly good, and some because they have fantastic marketing strategies. And of course some mediums are famous for both reasons: they are great *and* have great marketing professionals helping them. What you need to be careful of is the medium who has been well promoted but who does not have the skills to match the level of promotion and popularity.

If you are considering making an appointment for a private reading, get a recommendation from someone who has actually *had* a reading with the medium. If you are going to attend a demonstration, study chapter 6, "The Role You Play in Your Reading," and chapter 8, "Evaluating Your Reading." In these chapters you will learn how to understand and evaluate the evidence of survival that a medium brings. With this knowledge under your belt, you will be better able to tell a novice from a skilled medium even if the medium has a fabulous personality.

You will of course have to wait for a long time (sometimes years) for an appointment with an incredibly famous medium. When you have a special feeling about a very famous medium and really want to see that medium, then it may be worth the time you wait and the money you spend. Famous mediums such as John Edwards, Sylvia Browne, George Anderson, James von Prague, and Robert Brown have very long waiting lists.

Some well-known mediums will refer you to other mediums in the meantime, while you are waiting for your reading with them in a year or two. However, if a well-known medium makes a referral, you may want to find out if he or she has actually seen a demonstration by, or had a reading with, the medium to whom you are referred.

A friend of mine, John Holland, does a lot more work in large demonstrations in the United States than I do. I am not always available for demonstrations because I work quite a bit in other countries and also do many church services. As a result, he has a much longer waiting list than I have and refers people to me. But he has *seen me work* in many demonstrations.

Quite honestly, there are many mediums around the world whose skills are equal to those of the incredibly famous mediums, and I am sure that many famous mediums would agree with me. Not every medium wants to be famous and on the road all the time. Some highly talented mediums keep themselves sort of tucked away, to protect their privacy. I am grateful to those famous mediums who *are* willing to do the job of being famous, as they have brought spirit communication to the attention of millions of people. Books by famous mediums have also taught many people about mediumship. I grew up around people who were very famous, and it is not always an easy life, so I express my appreciation to the famous mediums who are teaching millions of people about spirit communication.

I am also grateful to mediums such as Tony Santos who are willing to share their large public demonstrations with other mediums, to give the public and good mediums an opportunity to meet each other. Tony's organization, The Other Side, promotes many classes and demonstrations of mediumship on his Web site *www.tonysantos.com.*

Phone Readings and 1-800 Numbers

I have to be honest and say that I have mixed feelings about phone readings of any kind. As I share the pros and cons of phone readings, you will see why I feel in conflict, as both the disadvantages and advantages are very credible.

THE DISADVANTAGES

The main reason I don't like phone readings is that they can never be as personal as a face-to-face reading. Particularly when the client may be in grief, the compassion of the medium and the healing that a very spiritual medium is able to bring to the reading can never be the same on the phone. Of course if a medium gives a reading over the phone to a client whom she has met with before, then the reader and the readee know each other a bit, and the reading may have a more personal quality. When I get a reading, I prefer to have a reading with a medium in person, and as a medium, I prefer to give readings in person.

I often do phone readings for people who cannot travel to my reading room. Sometimes clients of mine have relatives who want readings but live halfway across the United States or around the world, and cannot travel to me. I will also accept appointments with those who see my name listed in Web sites, but I like to have a brief conversation with them before making an appointment. However, I avoid really learning anything about them in these introductory conversations, as I do not want to have any prior knowledge of those I read for. But I can talk with prospective clients about how I work and answer any questions they have about spirit communication in general. This brief introductory conversation makes me feel that the phone reading will be a bit more personal.

THE ADVANTAGES

I was chatting with Bob Olson, the creator of two Web sites called *OfSpirit.com* and *BestPsychicMediums.com*. Bob and I were discussing the pros and cons of phone readings, and he really turned my head around in some ways and made me appreciate that a phone reading has the possibility of being more evidential than an "in person" reading. Think about it. If you call a medium on the telephone, that medium knows nothing about you. It is impossible for the medium to pick up any cues from your physical size, your age, coloring, or the way you are dressed.

Bob said to me, "Carole Lynne, you are a medium, and so you may not hear people express their anxieties about mediums as much as I do." He told me that some people are very anxious that the medium will somehow get information about them before the reading. He finds that these people are often more comfortable with a reading over the phone with a medium who is a complete stranger and who cannot even see them.

While a phone reading cannot provide the personal environment of the "in-person" reading, it does offer a situation in which both the medium and the client are protected from the medium's being influenced consciously or unconsciously by what she would observe if the client were present. In fact, when tests of mediumship are being done, a screen is often placed between the reader and the readee, so that the medium cannot see the client.

Having Weighed the Pros and Cons

I still prefer to do readings in person and advise you to get readings in person when you can. While any medium may at times unconsciously pick up cues, a well-trained medium will be able to bring you lots of good evidential information that she could never pick up just from seeing you in person. For instance, if a medium brings a message from your sister Lucy in the world of spirit, nothing about your appearance could have told the medium your sister's name. If the medium tells you that your sister Lucy passed with a particular disease and at a particular age, nothing about your appearance could have told the medium that.

So there is a great deal of information that a medium can receive in person that cannot be influenced by the medium's being able to see the client. Bob Olson and I will most likely be debating this topic for years to come, and he did make some very good points!

A Better Medium Is a Better Medium, on or off the Phone

I value a reading with a great medium over the phone more than a poor reading with a medium "in person." Again, we come back to the same truth, that what counts is not the place, or even whether or not you use a phone: it is the ability of the particular medium that is most important. A medium on the phone or off the phone must bring lots of good evidence so that both you and the medium can *know* the medium is really in communication with your loved one.

The 1-800 Numbers

These days, mediums sometimes are available through 1-800 numbers. This has usually been more the territory for psychics, but as the public is becoming more interested in spirit communication, mediums are also using these formats to reach those who want readings. You will find these services advertised in magazines and newspapers, on radio, television, and Web sites on the Internet. Readings are given over the telephone, and a fee is charged by the minute to your credit card.

For weeks and weeks I kept saying to myself, "I will call a 1-800 number for a reading tomorrow." I have not been able to get myself to do it. While I know that many people call these numbers for readings, and I am sure that there are some very good readers, I don't feel comfortable with this way of finding a medium or any other kind of reader. I need to either see a medium in a demonstration, get a good recommendation, or read about a medium in a newspaper, magazine, or Web site that specializes in researching mediums. So as your coach I'm afraid that I just can't help you with this one! You will have to be on your own if you want to check out the 1-800 numbers.

Internet Web Sites

There are Web sites devoted to the subject of spirit communication. Web sites are offered by Spiritualist organizations, individual churches, bookstores, spiritual centers, and individual mediums. There are Web sites that list many mediums who pay to have their names and profiles listed.

Bob Olson is *not* a medium but has readings with mediums and then recommends those who he thinks are evidential mediums on his Web site *www.BestPsychicMediums.com*. While any medium may be listed on *www.OfSpirit.com*, only those whose work Bob knows and *recommends* are listed on *www.BestPsychicMediums.com*. While these mediums do pay a fee to be listed, they are being recommended by the site after being evaluated.

Tony Santos's organization, The Other Side, found on the Internet at *www.tonysantos.com*, promotes demonstrations of mediumship and classes. There is also a very informative section on the site called "Frequently Asked Questions." Such questions as "What is mediumship and its purpose?" and "What happens if someone I do not want to speak to comes through?" are answered from Tony's perspective.

Mediums listed on Web sites provide contact information so that you can call or e-mail a medium to make either an in-person or telephone appointment. Some mediums are even giving readings on line, but this practice is not widespread at the moment. Method of payment will be discussed with the particular medium. Mediums normally have already paid a fee to be listed on Web sites, and so the fee you pay the medium will go to the medium.

WHERE TO FIND AN
ASTROLOGER OR PSYCHIC READER

A great deal of what has been said about finding a good medium can apply to finding an astrologer or psychic reader. However, the astrologer and the psychic do not do demonstrations in Spiritualist churches, and I have not ever heard of an astrologer doing a demonstration of astrology for a group. Most psychic and astrological work is done one-on-one.

Many astrologers advertise in spiritual magazines, as do many full-time psychics. Spiritual bookstores and centers also feature both of these kinds of readers, and you will find not only readings but also classes offered in the brochures that are sent out by these establishments every few months.

Because most psychic and astrological work is one-on-one, the best way to find a good astrologer or psychic is through a personal recommendation from a friend who has had a reading.

BEFORE YOU DECIDE ON A MEDIUM

I have described the places to find a medium, hopefully without too much bias. As your coach, I want you to know what all the options are. However, I also want to share my thoughts about each option with you. As I have suggested before, how and where you decide to find a medium should take into consideration whether you are just curious or if you are experiencing the grief of losing a loved one. How you find a medium, or any other kind of reader, should also depend on your experience as a readee.

Consider Your Level of Experience

If you are a new readee and have never had a reading, or if you have only had a couple of readings, I would encourage you to go slowly and make the safest choices as you look for a medium. Many people do not realize how emotional a reading with a medium can become. Some people, who think they are only curious about readings and almost treat the whole experience as a joke, find out that a reading with a medium is serious business. The safest way for a beginning readee to find a good medium is to select a medium who is educated and experienced.

Personally, I like to have readings with mediums who have been educated in mediumship. While the gift of mediumship is a natural gift, students of mediumship have to learn how to present the images they get of spirit in a manner that can be understood by others. Student mediums also need to learn how to treat their clients, who are often coping with feelings of grief.

Mediums are trained by Spiritualist organizations such as the American Federation of Spiritualist Churches, the National Spiritualist Association of Churches, and, in Great Britain, the Spiritualist National Union. There are additional spiritual groups and organizations dedicated to spirit communication, but as I have not had direct experiences with these organizations I prefer not to write about them from hearsay, good or bad. There are also good independent teachers of mediumship who were originally trained by schools and organizations dedicated to the education of mediums.

If you are brand-new to the world of mediums and readings, then you may want to pay attention to a recommendation from someone who has been around this world a lot longer than you. Even if you have seen a demonstration of mediumship that you think is incredible, you may not know yet *how* to listen to mediumship. A medium who impresses you now may not even strike you as particularly good a year from now, when you know more about evaluating mediumship. This medium may have a wonderful personality and great stage presence, but not bring very good evidence that the spirit is actually communicating. If you are a beginning readee, it may be a good idea to trust recommendations from an experienced medium rather your own impressions, until you've gotten your feet wet.

Consider Your Needs

While a person who is just curious about spirit communication may be able to handle almost any reader, a person who is grieving may be terribly upset by a medium who is treating the death of a loved one all too casually. I am sorry to say that there are mediums both within Spiritualism and without who are not well trained and may not be the best readers, especially for those who are in grief. While these readers may be able to get great evidence during a reading, not all are mature in the way that they deal with people in grief. Some younger mediums may have never lost a loved one and simply do not know what it feels like. You need a very good medium who is also a mature person—if not in age, in attitude.

Ask for Recommendations

Getting a recommendation is not only important for those who are inexperienced and those who are in grief, but for anyone who wants a reading. While attending a demonstration of mediumship may be the best way to find a good medium, the second best way is to get a recommendation from a friend, organization, church, or other medium. The reason I say "second best way" is that the medium someone else likes may not be a medium you will like. You need to feel comfortable with the medium you sit with, and so of course if you are able to watch a medium do a demonstration, this is an even better option.

Is It a Real Recommendation?

When I talk about a recommendation, I mean a referral from someone who has actually *had* a reading with a particular medium. Or I am talking about an organization that makes recommendations of those mediums they have educated and tested. If you get the name of a medium from a list of mediums, find out what it takes for a medium's name to be placed on that list. Are the mediums themselves paying for advertising, or is this a list of recommendations by a reputable organization? Being *listed* is one thing, and being *recommended* is quite another matter!

Sometimes Your Intuition Is Your Best Guide

As your coach, I want to tell you that you have come a long way. You know where and how to find a good medium. However, there may be times when you will find a good medium unexpectedly. Circumstances may develop in which you have been thinking about seeing a medium, and then all of a sudden you will meet a medium at a party, or your best friend will suddenly tell you about a reading that she had with a medium. If you have a strong feeling that you should make an appointment with that medium, make an appointment. Sometimes the right medium just appears right in front of us, and we should pay attention. On the other hand if you meet or hear about a medium and you don't have a good feeling about it, don't make the appointment even if you have researched the situation for months.

I find that when I create a balance in my life by using both logical common sense and mystical intuition, I get the best results. So study all the options for finding a medium that I have given you, and let your mystical intuition guide you as well.

CHAPTER FIVE

How Long Is a Reading, and What Does It Cost?

Y ou have done your homework: In chapter 3 you learned the difference between mediumistic, psychic, astrological, and card readings. Then in chapter 4 you learned where to find a good medium. In this chapter you will learn about the time and money issues related to mediumship. How long are readings, and what do they cost? I will not quote any exact prices, but I will describe readings of different lengths, from the shortest to the longest, and give you my opinion on the fees that mediums charge.

Readings of Different Lengths

These days, you can get readings that last from ten minutes to two or three hours. Some bookstores even advertise readings for a dollar a minute.

The Ten-to-Fifteen-Minute Reading

If you just want to "check out" what it is like to get a reading, this might be an option, but there are some real dangers to watch out for, unless the medium is not reading for profit. When a medium is giving short readings as a fundraiser for a church or other spiritual organization, she is not being paid. When a reader is giving many short readings, and this is her way of supporting herself, conflicts can develop between your needs and the reader's.

The Reader-Readee Cat and Mouse Game

Don't sign up for a ten-minute reading in a bookstore unless the reader is booked up after your appointment, or unless you are prepared to make it clear at the beginning that you only want a ten-minute reading. When the reader has nothing to do after your ten minutes, the reading can turn into a mind game between you and the medium. In other words, the reader is sitting there wondering if you will be willing to extend the reading. You are sitting there trying to decide if this is a good reader and if you want to pay for more time. The whole experience can become a contest of wills that ruins the reading. Neither you nor the medium should be concentrating on such thoughts—both of you should be involved in the reading.

Personally, I have had terrible experiences receiving readings when I asked for a ten-minute reading, only to have the reader say, "Okay, I will read for ten minutes, and then I'll charge you a dollar a minute for as many additional minutes as we spend." Suddenly, for me, the whole atmosphere is ruined. I feel as if I am playing a video game or a pinball machine, and I have to drop quarters in the slot in order to keep playing. I also feel that I will insult the reader if I do not extend my time. I become worried that I won't get a good reading unless I show signs that I may extend the session. Suddenly I am worrying instead of getting involved in the reading.

Of course, there are readers who do short readings and do not behave this way. But to be on the safe side, if you want a short reading, put your money down and tell the reader in a nice way that you are only going to stay as long as you have paid for. "Please don't be insulted if I don't extend the time of the reading. I have ten minutes available for this reading, and ten dollars to spend, and that is all today. Perhaps I will see you again on another day." This statement lets the reader know that she can concentrate on the reading and not waste any energy trying to get you to stay longer. If she does a good reading, hey, you might come back, or you can even change your mind and stay longer. You do have the right to change your mind, after all, but don't start out with that intention and set the stage for a reading that may become a cat and mouse game between you and the reader.

IF YOU ARE IN GRIEF

I advise those who are grieving or upset to avoid having a ten-to-fifteen-minute reading with a medium. You are better off saving your money and having a longer, more beneficial reading—I would say that twenty minutes should be the shortest, and half an hour to an hour would be preferable. When you are in grief, you do not need to have a reader abruptly end a reading after ten minutes.

Quite frankly, most good mediums will not give such short readings unless they are doing fundraisers for churches and spiritual centers or giving short readings at holistic fairs, where potential customers have an opportunity to have a short reading in order to get to know the work of the reader.

The Half-Hour to One-Hour Reading

I think that this is the best range of time for most readings of any kind. When a reader has at least half an hour, she is able to bring you lots of information, and if the reading lasts forty-five minutes to an hour, that is even better. Personally, when I work in my own reading room, I only give hour-long readings. I don't want to have to rush a client, and an hour allows the readee time to settle down before the reading and to ask questions or share thoughts afterward. Phone readings may be slightly shorter, as no time is taken up by arriving and departing, and I will give shorter readings as fundraisers for churches and spiritual centers.

When you make an appointment for a half-hour to one-hour reading, you will most likely be seeing a reader who books appointments in advance. This is not normally a "walk-in" kind of reading.

Readings Over One Hour

Most readings are not over an hour, but some readers, such as astrologers, feel that they cannot cover the necessary material in an hour's time. There are also mediums and psychics who prefer to see a client only once a year for an in-depth reading that will take over an hour, possibly up to two hours. I have even heard of a psychic who will only see a readee *once*, and for *four hours*. That is it. Whatever she has to tell you, she says it in four hours, and that is it for your lifetime!

I can see the value of the longer reading, particularly for the astrologer. There are charts to go over, and, depending on how many years you have lived, there may be a lot to talk about in terms of what has happened in the past.

However, you should be aware that if you make an appointment for a two-hour reading, you are going to spend some serious money. I would advise that you only do so when you have a referral, with great feedback, from someone who has personally experienced the medium's work. Nancy Garber in the Boston area does two-hour readings. She takes the time to bring many communicating spirits, and a reading with Nancy is very complete and evidential. She really cares about her clients. I have known her to go over the time allotted to listen to someone who is in grief—and to call a grieving client the next day just to say, "Hello, and how are you today?" From a medium who's dedicated to giving you a good reading, you will get your money's worth.

What Time Is It?

When making an appointment for a reading, ask for a time before the reader's last appointments of the day. Readers who are working for eight hours straight often do not know who they are at the end of the day, much less who you are and what messages there are for you. I am exaggerating, of course, but my point is that you don't want to be the first or last reading of the day. Personally, I prefer to book a reading so that I am about the third or fourth person a reader will be seeing that day. I don't want to have my reading when the reader is just finishing a first cup of coffee or herbal tea, *and* I don't want my reading at the end of the day, when the reader may be tired.

When making an appointment with a very busy and well-recommended medium, try to avoid the first or last appointment of the day, but don't be *too* picky. You may not have the luxury of getting an appointment at a specific time—in fact, you may be lucky to get an appointment at all.

How Much Mediums Charge and Why

When you call for an appointment, please, please, *please,* do not ask about the price first! Many of us care a great deal about the work that we do, and we feel insulted when the first question we hear over the telephone is, "What do you charge?"

If you are on a tight budget, I understand that you may not want to spend ten minutes on the phone with a medium, only to find out that you cannot afford the reading. But it is to your advantage to spend time on the phone with a medium, even if you don't end up making an appointment with that particular reader. You will learn a lot from the conversation, and if that medium is not the right reader for you, she may give you the name of a reader who *will* fit your needs. Many professional and well-known readers have students who will do practice readings at no charge or for a small fee. If you have made a bad impression on her by asking about the fee first, she may not want to send you off to one of her students or best friends who charges a lower fee.

Readings for No Charge

"Student mediums" often do readings for no charge. I have had some absolutely wonderful readings with students. There are also some mediums who feel that giving readings is such a spiritual act that there should be no charge. As I mentioned in chapter 4, there are some Spiritualist ministers who do not charge for readings. However, free readings are few and far between, and you should expect to pay a fee unless you really cannot afford one.

Some mediums who normally charge a fee will do readings for free for a person who is in real need of a reading and has genuine financial difficulties. Some Spiritualist mediums have told the pastors of Spiritualist churches that if there is anyone who cannot afford a reading, they will do a reading for free. But *please* do not ask a reader for a free reading and then go out to dinner with your friends! Many of us have done free readings for people, only to find out that we have been taken advantage of. If you are having trouble putting food on your table and paying your rent, then you might ask for a reading without payment. But if you can afford to go to the movies, eat out, and take vacations, then it is more responsible of you to make a choice and give up a few evenings out in order to have a reading.

You may not hear about it, but sometimes the well-known, high-priced mediums also give free readings to people in need. Internationally famous mediums cannot let the word get around that they occasionally read for free, however, or they will have hundreds of people asking for free readings. I also know that many of us have asked a mother who has just lost a child if she would like to give a donation to charity instead of paying a fee for the reading. It is heartbreaking to do a reading for a bereaved parent, and many times we have donated the fee to charity instead of being paid. I share this with you because professional mediums are often criticized for taking payment, even though they have bills like everyone else.

Inexpensive Readings

The prices of readings will vary in Spiritualist churches, spiritual centers, and spiritual bookstores, but should be fairly reasonable. Most of the readers in these settings will be trained and experienced. Most likely, they will not be famous, but that does not mean that they are not as good as some of the famous readers. There are readers who may not want to devote all their time to doing readings, as they have other jobs, other interests, or families to raise. There are readers who consider that fame and fortune are not appropriate for spiritual readings. It is important to such readers that they be available to the public at a reasonable rate.

Bookstores and spiritual centers want you to come into their locations not only for readings but also to buy other products and to sign up for courses and workshops. It is to their advantage to keep their fees for readings reasonable to bring in more people.

Spiritualist churches want to make sure that everyone can have a reading, so they always have reasonable prices or offer readings free of charge.

Fees of Full-Time, Professional Mediums

You can expect to pay a professional medium the kind of fee a therapist, dentist, or business consultant might charge for an appointment. Many people are critical of mediums charging such prices because they are doing "spiritual work." But you have to realize that all the spirituality in the world does not pay the mortgage, phone bill, car payment, or contribution to a retirement fund. Full-time mediums are self-employed. They have marketing costs, office expenses, and so on and so forth. If they don't charge a professional rate, they cannot give up working at other jobs to be full-time readers. They have to save money for a rainy day and their retirement, just like everybody else, and they do not work for a company that pays for their health insurance. Individual rates for health insurance can be very high.

Many full-time mediums I know feel conflicted about having to charge the same kind of professional rates as other people who make one-on-one appointments. But if professional full-time readers don't make enough money to lead reasonably comfortable lives, they will have to give up being readers—and there is a tremendous lack of good mediums. Many of the more expensive professional readers are very good and extremely committed to being mediums.

It is also important to understand that mediums cannot do readings forty hours a week. They can only do so many readings and keep up the quality of the readings. Besides doing readings, they have to spend time dealing with correspondence, setting up schedules, keeping tax records, and doing all the other tasks involved in having your own business. I would rather have good mediums, who charge what they must in order to stay in business, than have even fewer good mediums. So save up, if necessary, and please pay their fees.

ARE EXPENSIVE, FULL-TIME MEDIUMS BETTER THAN PART-TIME MEDIUMS?

Some people say that full-time mediums must be better, because they can attract enough clients to be able to read full-time. There is some truth to that point of view, but I have known full-time mediums who were not very good—they drew many clients because of their good looks or charismatic personality. You simply cannot generalize. If a medium is good, the medium is good, and it does not matter if she works full-time or part-time or works for free, charges a modest amount, or expects a professional fee.

Fees of the Rich and Famous Mediums

Expect to pay through the nose, as they say, for famous mediums. Famous people have to run even larger offices and have incredible expenses, so you are going to pay top prices for their services.

As I've said, some of these mediums may have exceptional talent and be worth every penny, while others benefit from a great publicity agent and a stroke of good luck. Personally, I would not get a reading from a famous person without receiving a referral from someone who'd had a good reading with that medium, or witnessing an impressive public demonstration given by the medium. In other words, I would not make an appointment for a reading *just because* the reader is famous. I would still need to feel that this is the right medium for me.

Quite frankly, some people want to have a reading with a famous medium because it is a status symbol for them to say, "I had a reading with so and so." At other times, people are in such desperate situations, or grieving so hard for the loss of a loved one, that they believe the famous medium is the only one who can help them. They feel that they want "the very best," and for them the best is the most famous and the most expensive. I am not a good person to try to impress when it comes to talk of fame. Having grown up in a family where I knew or heard about many famous people, I have found that fame is not what makes a person good or bad. Some of the famous people I knew were terrific, and some were not. The guy who ran the deli in my neighborhood was one of the best people around, and he never had a moment of fame—not even Andy Warhol's fifteen minutes. He always had a big, *genuine* smile for everyone who walked in his deli. He is in the world of spirit now, and I will never forget his pastrami sandwich. If there are delis in the world of spirit, I will find him someday.

If you really want the reading with the incredibly famous medium, save up and pay for it! If you have seen a demonstration by a famous medium and really want to have a reading with that person, wait for an appointment and spend the money. Sometimes we have a special feeling about someone, and we should honor that feeling.

As you can see, there are all kinds of places to find readings that range from ten minutes to several hours in length. There is also a wide range of fees. If you want a reading, you can have one. However, remember that you are not going out to buy soap, clothing, or dinner for two. In a reading with a medium you will be communicating with the spirits of your loved ones. Get the best reading you can.

CHAPTER SIX

THE ROLE YOU PLAY IN YOUR READING

ou have done your research, and you're ready. You have, or will soon have, an appointment for a reading with a medium. Bravo! As your coach, I would like to tell you that you have done a great job. You are going to see a medium for the *right* reasons.

Now it is time for you to learn how your attitude will influence the experience of a reading. You will also learn how to listen intelligently to the evidence that the medium will bring during your reading.

Although it is important that you know how your behavior can influence the success of your reading, please don't worry about becoming the perfect readee! Read this chapter, but do not take it so seriously that you are nervous during your reading. Those of you who are perfectionists could be so busy trying to "do it right" that you won't experience the reading itself. I am a perfectionist from way back, so I know what it's like.

REFRESH YOUR MEMORY

If you have taken the advice from chapter 2 and learned a bit more about the people in your family, refresh your memory before you go to your appointment with a medium. Review the names of those family members that you didn't know too well. Those who were very close to you will not be hard for you to recognize from the descriptions the medium gives you. You know so much about them that there will be many things the medium can say about them that will immediately be familiar to you.

There may also be some communicating spirits whom you were not so close to.

Let's say you had a cousin named Rachel who lived in Colorado. The medium says to you, "I have a woman here, and her name begins with the letter *R*. I feel that she is a cousin of yours and that she is from out west someplace." If you've researched your relatives, then instead of taking fifteen minutes to figure out whom the medium is talking about, you will say, "That is my cousin Rachel from Colorado." Now the medium will be able to continue with the reading. While you may be happy to hear from your cousin Rachel, there may be other loved ones in spirit whom you would like to hear from. If you and the medium have to spend a lot of time trying to figure out who this cousin with the initial *R* is, there will be less time left for the medium to receive impressions from others who may be "waiting in line" to speak with you.

Remember:
Do Not Tell the Medium Anything!

As you arrive for your reading, remind yourself not to say anything as you walk in the door. I know I have already told you this before, but even we mediums have to remind each other not to tell too much when we are going to have a reading with another medium! So, as you get ready to go your appointment, it is time to play those instructions over and over in your mind again, because many people are excited and nervous when they walk into a session with a medium. It is easy to blurt out something like, "My grandfather has just died of heart failure, and I really hope he comes through in this reading. I had such a great relationship with him, and I miss him so much. To make matters worse, my best friend just passed away this fall." When this happens in my reading room, I have to rudely interrupt people and yell, "*Be quiet!* I don't want you to tell me anything more!"

I repeat: A reputable medium will want to know as little about you as possible. If the medium has heard nothing about your grandfather, but describes a man who looks like him and who has recently passed with heart failure, both you and the medium will be much more convinced that he has actually come through in the reading. If the medium brings this information along with additional evidence about the personality of your grandfather, perhaps his first name or the initial of the name, and something about the quality of your relationship to him, you will know that the spirit of your grandfather is there. Both you and the medium can be certain that the information did not come from some comment you made as you entered the room.

UNDERSTANDING THE MEDIUM'S EVIDENCE

The more you understand about the evidence that a medium brings, the better you will be able to take part in a reading with a medium. There are several things about evidence for you to consider.

- It is not any one piece of evidence, but the accumulation of evidence that gives us a picture of the spirit.
- Sometimes a medium's interpretation of personality may be different from yours.

- Be open to hearing from whoever comes from the world of spirit. Those who go to a reading insisting that a particular spirit will come through may be disappointed.
- Be open to whatever the communicating spirit has to say to you.
- Sometimes the evidence is amazing, inspiring, and absolutely convincing and sometimes it's not.

Let's look at each of these points separately.

The Accumulation of Evidence Gives Us a Picture of the Spirit

No one piece of evidence proves that a particular spirit is there, not even a name. If a medium says, "I have a man in spirit named 'Bob' here," that is not enough. Obviously there are plenty of people named Bob in this world, and the chances are that most of us know someone named Bob who is in spirit.

But if the medium not only says, "I have Bob here," but adds the fact that Bob was heavy during his lifetime but lost a lot of weight before passing from cancer, *and* that he passed in his fifties, *and* he was usually a nice guy but was known to have a terrible temper on occasion, *and* he did the kind of work where he sat behind a desk most of the day, *and* that he had a dog and a pet parrot, *now* we are beginning to have enough evidence to know that this is the spirit of *your* Bob. It is unlikely that there is any other man named Bob that you know, who is in spirit, and of whom all those facts are true. Many people do not work behind a desk, many people don't die of cancer, and very few people that you know named Bob, who have passed on, had both a dog and a pet parrot. And while there may be people you know who do each of those things mentioned, it is the fact that *all* of the evidence is true of the Bob that you know.

Please do not dismiss the spirit of Bob if there is only *one* piece of evidence that is not totally correct. Mediums can interpret things incorrectly and make a slight mistake. For instance, in the case of Bob, the medium said that Bob worked behind a desk most of the time. Maybe Bob showed an image to the medium of himself sitting behind a desk, but in truth he only spent *half* of his time sitting behind the desk and the rest of his time traveling to other branches of his office. You, the readee, have a choice. You can say "No, Bob did not spend most of his time behind a desk, and I know for a fact that he traveled often to branch offices. So that is not Bob." If you want to be that picky, you may end up sending the spirit of Bob away, or spending your whole reading arguing with the medium as to whether Bob spent *most* of his time, or only *half* of his time behind a desk.

But if you find that almost all of the evidence is on the mark, and only this one piece of evidence is not quite correct, you can say, instead, "Most of the evidence you have brought is correct, including the fact that Bob had a pet parrot, which is of course an unusual piece of evidence. And I can see that Bob might show you an image of himself behind a desk, as he did work behind a desk quite often, but not *most* of the time. Everything is absolutely correct except that one small detail, so I accept that this is Bob, and I would like to know what more he has to say." It's up to you.

I wish to make it very clear that I am not advising you to accept that the spirit of Bob is communicating if you feel that *much* of the evidence is incorrect—but if one piece is slightly incorrect, do you really want to dismiss the spirit of your loved one? Many mediums will stop communicating with a spirit if the spirit cannot be identified. For some mediums, giving you a message from a spirit who has not been identified would be like delivering an unsigned letter to you that had been thrust into their hands with a delivery request.

If you want to hear from your loved ones in the world of spirit, you may not want to spend your whole reading dissecting every little bit of evidence. I have sat with people who argued over whether there were two or three stones in a ring their mother wore, during a reading in which we had Mom's first name correct, cause of death correct, and the number of Mom's sisters correct. This readee had so much specific evidence that it seemed silly to me to argue about two or three stones. I do not mind admitting that I could perceive that ring incorrectly. As a medium, I am ready to accept that a spirit is identified if *most* of the very specific evidence is correct.

I also have compassion for the communicating spirit who may have spent years waiting for an opportunity to speak through a medium. I hate to dismiss all the good evidence that has been brought and, in effect, send that spirit away unrecognized because one piece of evidence is not perfect.

A Medium's Interpretation of Personality May Be Different from Yours

As I greet a loved one of yours from the world of spirit, I may respond to the spirit's personality differently than you responded to this person when he was alive. When I perceive the communicating spirit during a reading, it is as if I am meeting someone for the first time. I get a "first impression" of the personality.

For instance, suppose I bring the spirit of Aunt Mary to you and tell you that as I perceive Aunt Mary she was very "playful." As I perceive Aunt Mary in spirit, I see that she is dancing around having a good old time, and I *get the impression* that the family must have enjoyed her. As the medium, I am experiencing Aunt Mary in a positive manner. You, the readee, tell me that Aunt Mary was a binge drinker who drove the family crazy, and she was *not* a lot of fun and playful! Then I tell you that the image I am perceiving of Aunt Mary in one in which Aunt Mary is dancing around. You say, "Well, now that I think of it, she did use to dance around and sing when she was drunk." Okay, so what we have here is an example of how a medium can bring an *image* that is true but an *interpretation* that is not correct. The image of Aunt Mary dancing is correct, but my interpretation that the family must have enjoyed her is *not* correct.

However, if in this reading, I have brought lots of information about Aunt Mary that is absolutely correct, it would be a shame to decide that this is *not* Aunt Mary because an interpretation has been incorrect. A wise and experienced readee would be able to say to me, "It was not all quite the way you see it, but I understand from what you see *why* you could come to that conclusion." In this instance, I am able to continue with the reading and give a message from Aunt Mary, and perhaps from others who are waiting to communicate.

Be Open to Hearing from Whoever Comes from the World of Spirit

If you assume that any descriptions I bring will be of your Aunt Sally, and I am describing your sister Lucy, then you are not going to understand any of the evidence I am bringing. If I say, "I have a woman here in spirit who has blond hair," and Aunt Sally had black hair, then you will not recognize what I am saying. Instead of believing that you know which spirit will communicate, you need to wait until I bring you five, ten, maybe fifteen to twenty pieces of information about a spirit who is trying to communicate—*then* you can think of everyone you know who has passed into the world of spirit and identify which person I am describing.

Unfortunately, I have no control over which spirits will come through. When my mother passed into the world of spirit, it was a couple of years before I got a communication from her. I had many readings over the three years after she passed, and while my father came through, as well as a good friend of mine, my mother did not. I heard *about* my mother from Dad, who is in spirit, but she did not come through. The mediums that I saw explained that sometimes it takes a while for a spirit to communicate. In the case of my mother, that proved to be true. It was Sondra Adelman, a student in one of my classes, who brought the message from my mother, and she was not even trying. As we sat in a circle meditating, the spirit of my mother came to her. Later in the class, when we were sharing our experiences with each other, Sondra said, "I am not a medium, but I just had this experience. I saw an image of a woman, and she . . ." Sondra went on to give a perfect description of my mother. So, we never know when and to whom a particular spirit is going to come through.

No matter how much you want to hear from your Grandma Helen, a good medium will never try to make your sister Sara into your grandmother just to make the evidence fit your expectations. And if you try to do so, by insisting that a communication *must* be from Grandma when the description suggests Sara, you will be kidding yourself. A reputable medium will insist on quite a bit of information before concluding *who* the spirit is, and she will try to help you be patient until there's enough evidence to identify a communicating spirit.

You, the readee, can be of great help to those who work as mediums, by understanding that we have no control over which spirits come through, or in what order they come through during your reading. Clients who become agitated when they don't get what they want in a reading can put pressure on a medium to tell them what they want to hear. Weaker-minded mediums may give in and lie about what they are receiving from spirit. There is *no* excuse for a medium to be dishonest, but *you*, the readee, need to be honest with yourself as well. While you may be disappointed at times, please let us know that you appreciate our honesty and integrity, and that you would never want us to be any other way.

As I've said before, I find that most of the time the spirits you expect to hear from will be the ones who communicate, but a reading will not always go the way you want it to go. Remember, you are at a reading where a medium is connecting with another dimension. You are not in a restaurant where you can say, "I would like an ice cream sundae with whipped cream on top, hold the cherries" and expect to get it!

Be Open to Whatever the Communicating Spirit Has to Say to You

Sorry, but you cannot write a script for the communicating spirit. I gave a reading the other day for a woman, and her brother came through from the world of spirit. The woman recognized her brother, but when the reading was over, she said, "That could not have been my brother. He kicked the hell out of me when I was a kid, and how could he possibly come through without an apology?"

It is very hard for the readee when a loved one from spirit comes through but does not say what the readee thinks the spirit would have or should have said. Why does this happen? Why did my client's brother not say what he was "supposed" to say?

In this case, the readee was expecting an apology from her brother in spirit. But maybe her brother was not ready to deliver an apology. Or it could be that he *was* delivering an apology, but I was not picking up on it. A communicating spirit sends many pieces of information to me during a reading, and I may not pick up on all of them. While that thought frustrates me a great deal, the reality is that I am communicating with a spirit in a different dimension—the reception is not always clear!

Now, I could make myself look better by saying that it was the fault of the brother, and he is a really bad person for not making an apology. But I would never say that because I cannot be sure that he didn't try to apologize. In my heart I believe that mediums do not receive every bit of information the communicating spirits send. The honest answer is that I do not know why an apology from the brother did not come through during the reading. There is still a great deal of mystery involved in spirit communication.

Sometimes the Evidence Is Amazing and Sometimes It's Not

Sometimes the medium will bring information about your relationship with your loved one that is so personal, unique, and special that there will be no doubt in your mind that the spirit of your loved one is communicating through the medium. Maybe the medium will bring a description of your loved one that is so correct, and rings so true, that it could be no one else. While you will not see the spirit of your loved one with your physical eyes, you may feel their presence in your heart. Those beautiful moments, where the evidence is so clear and the presence of spirit can be felt so deeply, are the moments that make most mediums willing to continue doing readings, and that keep many people like you coming back for more readings. Those are the special moments. For mediums, those are the moments when we know why we are *called* to do this work.

Unfortunately every reading is not like that. Sometimes we struggle to get a description of your loved one correct. Sometimes we see certain spirits more clearly than others. We debate with each other as to why this should be. Many of us believe that some spirits are able to communicate better than others. After all, that was true when all of these spirits were alive—some of them were more talkative than others. In fact, sometimes the fact that a communicating spirit does not have much to say is very evidential. The readee will say to me, "You know, that must be my friend Sam, because he never talked much, so I can understand that *is* Sam. He is behaving the way he always behaved."

And to be perfectly honest, some of us are much more evidential mediums than others. You will find a great range in the abilities of mediums to bring specific evidence. The *kind* of evidence that mediums bring varies from medium to medium. Some of us are much better at describing the personality, while others get more names. Some mediums are excellent at identifying how the spirit passed. The best of us are great at bringing *all* kinds of evidence. However, many of us are still learning and will become much better mediums every year that we continue to work. And, sadly, there are some who may believe they are communicating with spirit and call themselves mediums, who are really not linking with spirit. While I wish that *all* mediums could be of high quality, it is only fair to say that in *any* profession we will find people ranging from the highly gifted to the less than talented.

How Much Evidence Is Enough?

Some mediums are able to get the full name of your loved ones in spirit and even the address where they once lived. These mediums are few and far between. But when a medium is able to get such incredibly specific evidence, you will most likely be convinced.

As your coach, I do have to tell you that there are mediums who feel that more evidence is necessary, because the medium who picks up names and addresses may be picking them up from the readee, on a psychic level. To be sure that they are really in communication with the spirit, some mediums also require such evidence as a correct description of the spirit's personality and the dynamics of the relationship between the communicating spirit and the recipient of the message. They feel that such complex evidence would be difficult to pick up on a psychic level and is therefore more evidential of spirit communication than just a name and address alone. In other words, from this viewpoint, if a medium brought you the name and address of your mother who is in spirit, you would also want to hear about her personality and how you got along with her when she was alive.

However, if a medium does bring you a name and address, and you then start getting picky about the rest of the evidence, the medium may become understandably irritable! Personally, if any medium brought me the names and addresses of my loved ones in spirit, I would be eternally grateful, but I have tried to be honest with you in this book about *all* points of view, including those of mediums who do not find this sort of evidence as convincing as I do.

I cannot count the hours that I have spent discussing evidence with mediums. These discussions go on endlessly. For me, the best evidence is a collection of information of many different kinds. If a medium cannot bring me such convincing evidence as a full name and address, then I want to hear a description of the spirit, how the spirit passed, the name or first initial of the spirit, and—most important—the personality and behavior of the spirit. I also want to hear about how I related to the spirit. What did we share together?

I am one of the mediums who feel that a first name by itself does not mean a whole lot. I want to hear evidence about my loved one in spirit that feels "alive" to me. That is why I need to hear about personality and behavior. But there are mediums who feel differently. That is why we talk endlessly about evidence.

Your Role in the Reading

You play a very important role in the process of the reading—any kind of reading. Although the following advice refers to readings with a medium, your common sense will tell you where it can apply to all readings.

Your Attitude

It is the medium's responsibility to give you a good reading, no matter what kind of attitude you walk in with. Notice I am using the word "attitude," and not "mood." No one would want to dictate your mood, but you can decide to have a good attitude about your reading. In mediumship classes, we are taught that we must not be affected by the attitude of the client, and that no matter how the client behaves we must strive to bring as much evidence as possible about the client's loved ones in spirit. That is true and it sounds good, or, as people say, "It looks good on paper." But we have feelings, and *of course* we are affected by your attitude. A friendly attitude on your part does a great deal to enhance the experience of a reading.

One reason that mediums are sensitive to the client's mood is that, throughout the ages, mediums have been treated like freaks, frauds, and weirdos. Unfortunately, there have been many fraudulent mediums, but there are also bankers, lawyers, doctors, and people of all professions who are frauds. I think mediums get more than their share of suspicion and criticism. The fact is that most of us are caring individuals who never set out to be mediums. Many of us, because of the experiences we have had seeing spirits, feel that it is our responsibility to share this gift with the world.

Most of us are sincere mediums and only want to give you the very best reading that we can. Give us a chance. I, and many other mediums I know, have given up more lucrative work to do readings for people who are yearning to hear from their loved ones in spirit. Yet sometimes those very people then "freak out" when we bring them convincing evidence, and say that we must have somehow found it out beforehand. It is often when we do our very best work that people claim it is a "setup." Sometimes the evidence is so specific that some people cannot believe that we have received such information from the world of spirit, and the only way they can explain it is to claim that we are frauds.

Many of us feel *called* to be mediums in the same way that ministers of many religions feel called. In fact, many mediums *are* ministers or certified mediums within the religion of Spiritualism. So come into the reading with an open heart. If you understand what makes us who we are, your attitude will help us give you the reading you need.

Your Emotions

Don't get upset if you cry! When your loved ones come in from the world of spirit, and when a medium can bring you the kind of specific evidence that lets you really *know* that they are there, it is normal to feel emotional. Many people cry. I am very happy for people who are able to recognize their loved ones in spirit and who feel comfortable enough to cry. Sometimes we all cry! As I communicate with those in the world of spirit, I sometimes see tears in their eyes also. It is an emotional meeting for them as well. I have the impression that there are spirits who have waited for years to have the opportunity to speak through a medium. If you are able to accept and express your emotions during a reading, it may help you to participate more fully in the experience.

When to Keep Your Information to Yourself

Are you there for a reading or a conversation? Some clients interrupt me so much that I wonder why they have come for a reading. They make it impossible for me to give them the evidence I am receiving. I say, "I have your mother here, and she—" and before I know it, the readee is telling me all about Mom, and there is nothing evidential left for me to bring. I understand that the readee is telling me all about Mom because she is excited and wants to share her stories with me. *But the whole purpose of the reading is for the medium to bring the evidence.* So if you are the talkative type, put masking tape over your mouth if you have to (only kidding!), but keep the facts to yourself. At the end of the reading, you may want to give the medium some feedback on the evidence that she has brought to you, and share some nice stories about your mother.

When to Talk

You *should* respond briefly to the information the medium brings. For instance, suppose I say to you, "I have your brother here in spirit, and I see that he used to ride a motorcycle." If this is true, you should say, "Yes, my brother *did* ride a motorcycle." But then be quiet. Don't say, "Yes, and he also ran a print shop down the road, and that is where he met his girlfriend, who eventually died a year after he did. Do you think she is in spirit with him?"

Your Expectations

You may not get what you asked for in a reading, but you may get what you need. Many of us have specific expectations and hopes as we go off to our first readings. I wish I could tell you that a reading will go the way you have planned it. But as your coach I have to be totally honest with you and tell you that a reading may or may not turn out the way you want it to be. But remember that life is like that anyway, as we deal with people who are living. If we can't control when living people are going to show up and what they are going to say, why do we think we should be able to control their behavior when they are in spirit? As I've emphasized before, you and the medium have no control over which spirits will communicate and what they will say. The more you can accept that reality, the better able you will be to take full advantage of what does happen in your reading.

I find that there is a spiritual "justice" in readings. I admit that I do not know how the spirits respond when I am going to give a reading. All I can say is that most people get what they need. Sometimes a spirit who was not expected will show up and give meaningful advice or even a message of profound importance to the sitter. And when the sitter is able to relax, let go of preconceptions, and take part in the reading, real healing often takes place. There is an energy and vibration in the room that is indescribable. Don't miss what may be a beautiful and life-changing experience because it does not play out the way you have imagined it will.

As your coach, I urge you to be discerning as you listen to the evidence in a reading. But I also hope that you can be open to sensing the presence of spirit in your heart.

CHAPTER SEVEN

GROUP DEMONSTRATIONS OF MEDIUMSHIP

From chapter 6, you have learned all about the evidence that a medium brings. You understand that you must be open to whoever comes from the world of spirit and to whatever they have to say. You may have already had a private reading with a medium, but some of you will wish to attend a demonstration of mediumship first. In chapter 4 you learned that demonstrations are a good place to find a good medium.

In this chapter you will learn more about how evidence is brought by the medium during a demonstration of mediumship. There are some real differences in format between a demonstration and a private reading. Since many of you may attend demonstrations in order to meet mediums with whom you would like to have private readings, it is important that you understand more about the ways mediums work with a group. However, *you do not have to completely understand how mediums work before seeing a demonstration*. Read the rest of the chapter, and then see several demonstrations. Understanding the ways mediums work in demonstrations takes a bit of experience.

A word of warning: Let me repeat, once again, that if you are in grief, please understand that you are not guaranteed a message when you attend a demonstration of mediumship. The larger the demonstration, the more the odds are against your receiving a message. Attending demonstrations is a great way to learn about spirit communication, but if you cannot accept the fact that you may not receive a message, then you belong in a private reading at this time.

CHOOSING A DEMONSTRATION

Consider the choices, and take your time. Each type of demonstration is different. As you know, Spiritualist churches have demonstrations of mediumship as part of their weekly religious service. Some bookstores and spiritual centers also have demonstrations. As the interest in spirit communication is becoming greater, promoters now organize large demonstrations in meeting rooms and concert halls that seat from one hundred to a thousand people. You need to decide which kind of group demonstration is right for you.

As your coach, it is important for me to advise you not to judge the value of spirit communication and demonstrations of mediumship by one demonstration. You should see at least six to twelve demonstrations by different mediums before coming to any conclusions. Some prefer mediums who are very reverent, while others prefer more entertaining mediums. Some of you will prefer the demonstration in a Spiritualist church, and some will prefer the larger public demonstration in a concert hall. The medium you like the most may be the medium I like the least, and vice versa—but if you are like me, you will find each setting valuable in its own way, so it may take some time to decide which one works best for you.

Within the community of mediums, we have many debates about the proper way for a medium to conduct a demonstration, and believe me when I tell you that we do not all agree! *People need to find the kind of setting that is most comfortable for them, and the mediums with whom they feel secure.* What is important is that those in the world of spirit have opportunities to speak to us through mediums.

Understanding the Terminology

Most of the terms used in a demonstration will be the same as those used in private readings, with a couple of additions. The person giving the demonstration is called the medium, and the spirits with whom the medium is linking will be called the communicating spirits, or the communicators. In a demonstration, however, you may hear a term that you won't hear much in private readings: the *recipient*. In a private reading, you are the only one who is receiving messages, so it is not necessary to identify you. But in a demonstration, the medium has anywhere from ten to one thousand people sitting in front of her—she not only has to link with the communicator, she also has to find out who, among all those present, is meant to receive the communicator's message.

Identifying the Recipient of the Message

Mediums identify the recipient in two different ways: the direct method and the indirect method. In the direct method, the medium goes *directly* to someone in the group and tells that person that there is a communicator present with a message. The medium who works the indirect method will first describe the communicator, while everyone in the group listens closely, and then ask, "Who recognizes this communicator?"

Of course, that was only a thumbnail sketch of both the direct and indirect methods. In order to for you to understand these methods, we need to take a closer look.

The Direct Method

The medium who works "direct" feels guided to go to a particular person and will look directly at that person and say something like, "I would like to talk to the lady sitting in the fourth row, wearing a red blouse. May I come to you with a message?" The lady in the red blouse either says, "Yes" or "No, I prefer not to receive a message." Frankly, in years of attending demonstrations, I have only seen a couple of people refuse messages, but it does happen. And anyone who does not want a message has a perfect right to say so!

If the lady in the red blouse has said yes, we now consider her "the recipient of the message." Now the medium gives the recipient evidence about the communicating spirit that she is seeing, hearing, or sensing. This may be evidence such as physical description, cause of death, profession, relationship to the recipient, and any other pertinent information that will help the recipient to recognize the communicating spirit. The medium might say something like, "I have a man here who was about six feet tall, and he tells me he was very strong in his younger days. He says he could lift heavy weights, and so he worked for a moving company when he was a teenager. This man has brown eyes and brown hair, and I sense that he had an injury in his right hip. I see the letter *H* next to him, so I feel that his first or last name begins with that letter. He comes close to you, and I sense that he is a relative. I am hearing the word 'brother' and sense that this is your brother in spirit."

After giving the evidence, the medium asks the recipient, "Do you understand?" What the medium is really asking is if the recipient knows who this spirit is, from the description that has just been given. The recipient will either say that she understands who this is, or that she does not. If the recipient does understand who the communicating spirit is, the medium will now give the recipient a message from the communicating spirit. In other words, the medium will tell the recipient why her brother has come and what he has to say. The medium might say, "Your brother is here today as he knows that you are concerned about the health of your mother, who is still living. He wants you to know that he is sending healing from the world of spirit." If the recipient's mother *is* still living, and the recipient *is* concerned about the health of her mother, then she and everyone in the room who has been listening to this message will know that the spirit is actually there communicating through the medium. This is what we call "proving survival." By bringing correct evidence about someone in the world of spirit—evidence that she had no knowledge of beforehand—the medium has proved that the spirit is living in the world of spirit, and therefore that we all survive the change called death.

If, on the other hand, the medium has given a great deal of information, and the recipient does *not* understand who the communicating spirit is, then the medium will try to get more information. Some mediums will ask, "Is there anyone sitting close to this lady who can understand all of this information?" Sometimes that is the case. The medium has not brought the information to the right person in the group, and must now thank the lady in the red blouse for working with her and take the message to the man sitting three seats away, who does understand all the information.

However, sometimes when a medium feels extremely certain that she is with the correct recipient, she will ask the recipient to think it over and see if she can place whom the medium is describing. A good medium will not have to do this very often. Most good mediums will be able to place most of their messages within a demonstration of mediumship. But it is not unusual for a medium to deliver eight messages during a demonstration and have one message that is not accepted by anyone. It could be that the medium is not describing the communicating spirit in a manner that can be understood by the recipient, or it could be that the recipient does not know the spirit who is communicating. Perhaps it is the grandmother the recipient never really knew.

The Indirect Method

When a medium is working with the indirect method, she will be linking with a communicating spirit but will not know to *whom* this spirit belongs. So instead of going directly to someone in the group, such as the lady with the red blouse, the medium will instead describe the communicating spirit first, and then ask if anyone in the group can understand who this is.

Let me give you an example of the indirect method. The medium says, "I have a lady here from the world of spirit. She tells me that her name is Lucy and that her daughter is sitting here in the group today. Lucy passed when she was in her seventies, from cancer. Does anyone here recognize this spirit?" Believe it or not, three people may raise their hands. In other words, there may be three people in the room who have a mother named Lucy in the world of spirit, who passed in her seventies from cancer. So the medium, seeing three hands raised, will have to go back to the communicating spirit of Lucy and get more information.

Now the spirit of Lucy tells the medium that she was a schoolteacher. The medium says to the three people who raised their hands,

"Lucy says that she was a schoolteacher." Two of the three raised hands go down, and there is one person who can now understand all the evidence that has been brought, as her mother Lucy *was* a schoolteacher. If the medium is really picky about evidence, she may want to get a few more pieces of information, just to make sure that she is with the correct recipient. Once she knows that she has the correct recipient, she will bring the message from the spirit of Lucy to her daughter.

Could you follow that? If not, you're not alone. Sometimes people get confused at first, because we are really dealing with communication in two dimensions—the life you and I call "reality," and the world of the spirit. That can take some getting used to! You could read the description of the indirect method again, or you could just go see a demonstration. What you have read will suddenly make sense to you as you actually see mediums in action. I cannot tell you how wonderful it is to witness a medium helping the spirits communicate messages to their loved ones. As a medium, I feel an incredible satisfaction when this happens, and it makes me want to teach everyone I know, including *you*, more about how spirit communication works.

The Direct Method versus the Indirect Method

There are pros and cons to each method, and, believe me, mediums debate these issues. Some mediums feel that it is much more evidential to work the indirect method, because linking *only* with the communicator allows no chance for the medium to pick up psychic energy from the recipient of the message. These mediums also feel that by linking with the communicator first, they will avoid being influenced by the looks or behavior of the recipient of the message.

Other mediums feel that if you don't know whom the message is for right away, then you are not worth your salt as a medium. They believe very strongly in the fact that the spirit will *tell* you who the recipient of the message is. Mediums who prefer the direct method also dislike the whole process that takes place when mediums who work the indirect method are faced with several people who recognize the same evidence. Then the medium has to get more and more evidence to find out who the true recipient of the message is, and the demonstration can develop a game show or contestlike atmosphere, as potential recipients are "eliminated."

But according to mediums who prefer to work indirectly, the fact that ten people in the group *can* recognize the same evidence is what makes it mandatory for the medium to get very specific evidence that only *one* person in the whole room will be able to recognize—making it a much more evidential method.

But people who dislike the indirect method say that the more people there are in the room, the more the odds are that someone will recognize the evidence, no matter how specific. They feel that it is much more evidential for the medium to *know* who is the intended recipient of the message in the first place.

Oh dear. Oh dear. This debate has kept me up until two in the morning, talking and rehashing the arguments on all sides of the issue. How do you think I work: with the direct method or the indirect?

If you have read this book right from the beginning, you are by now getting to know my personality. You are not necessarily psychic if you come up with the right answer: *I work both methods.* I went through a phase when I was absolutely convinced that the direct method was the only way to go. Then I went through a second stage when I felt that the indirect method was the right way. But I am an explorer and adventurer when it comes to mediumship. I have to keep pushing every method I work, and I have to keep trying to understand more about how and why we get the evidence we do. Today, there is no way I could give up either of these methods, because it feels to me as if the world of spirit wants to work with me in both ways.

Sometimes I am absolutely *sure* of who the recipient of the message is, and so I go directly to that person. There are other times when I hear spirit say to me, "This next message is going to be indirect," and so I work the indirect method. At this point, I do not make any decisions about how I am going to work. I work as I feel directed by spirit at the moment. And if I learn of any new method, I am willing to experiment before I decide that it is a good or bad way of working.

A Good Demonstration

No matter what method the medium uses, a good demonstration is an evidential demonstration. Good mediums will be consistently accurate in their descriptions of those communicating from the world of spirit. This means that the communicating spirits will be recognized by the recipients of the message, not *all*, but *most* of the time. In a demonstration, a medium should be able to give communication for an hour or so at a time, consistently. Giving an evidential message here or there does not demonstrate mediumship.

Good mediums will express themselves in a manner that is both caring and compassionate as they deliver messages to the recipients from their loved ones in spirit. They will conduct a demonstration with a dignified, healing attitude. These mediums will also know how to use just enough humor in a demonstration to keep people interested, but not so much as to compromise the dignity in what is a sacred communication.

Real mediums can also touch the heart by bringing us the closeness of spirit. Remember, those in the spirit world *want* to communicate with us. One way for mediums to do their part is by holding demonstrations that allow the communicating spirits to deliver their messages. You can do your part by attending demonstrations so that mediums can deliver those messages from those in the world of spirit. Give your loved ones in spirit an opportunity to communicate with you.

EVALUATING YOUR READING

You have had a reading. You have received a message during a private reading, or you have been fortunate enough to receive a message during a group demonstration. Perhaps you have been given some advice during this reading and are thinking about what has been said to you. How seriously should you take the message? Should you follow the advice or forget it?

Having a reading can be a profoundly moving experience for many of us. It is important for you to *stay in charge* and evaluate how much you wish to let the experience change your life. If you went to see any other kind of professional, you would evaluate the experience and not just follow advice without considering it carefully. It is just as important to evaluate a reading.

How Did the Reading Make You Feel?

Evaluate the way you are feeling after the reading. Has it affected you? How? Was it an uplifting experience, or was it anxiety producing? Do you feel more positive about your life? Did you come away from the experience with any new ideas? Or did you walk away from the reading feeling down and a bit depressed?

Besides being evidential, a good reading should have a healing effect. When I have had a good reading, I feel wonderful. Frankly, I am very sensitive, and if a reading does not have a healing quality, then I do not feel that I've experienced a good reading. The medium may not have spoken of "healing," but when a reader is kind, gentle, compassionate, and caring, she generates a quality of healing that one can almost touch. When a reader is patronizing, bossy, arrogant, or manipulative, then the whole quality of the reading can feel negative or depressing.

I do not mean to insinuate that every word said by the medium has to be happy and bright, or even positive. The medium who will leave me feeling positive may have related even sad and difficult things, but with a positive attitude. Of course, if I turn everything the reader says into a negative thought, I will not feel positive, even if the reader is the most positive and tactful person in the world. It is up to me as well as the reader to create a positive experience.

If you feel positive and uplifted, you may want to spend time understanding what it was about the reading that made you feel so good. Write a few notes in a journal so that you can remember the important aspects of the reading. And if you have taped the reading, replay the tape to reinforce the positive feelings.

If you do not leave a reading feeling that you had a positive experience, then you need to let go of that reading. Admit to yourself that you did not make a good choice, and try to forget the reading. I had a terrible experience in my twenties with a palm reader who had a mysterious and somewhat negative attitude. To be honest, the reading haunted me for years. It was not any bad predictions that the reader brought, but just an attitude that "spooked me." Finally, years later, I have let go of that experience. It did, however, teach me a lesson, and I am very choosy about whom I will get *any kind* of reading from.

Should You Follow the Advice You Receive During a Reading?

Always evaluate advice given to you in a reading before following it—no matter where it comes from.

Advice from a Loved One

In a mediumistic reading, the loved ones in spirit who communicate may give you advice, but always evaluate *any* advice with respect to who gave it, even advice from a loved one in spirit. Remember, if you didn't follow the advice of brother Bob *before* he passed, don't follow his advice now just because he is in spirit! While most mediums feel that spirits advance when they enter the realm of spirit, we do not feel that they become infallible beings. As a Spiritualist medium and minister, I have come to understand that each one of us makes a transition to the world of spirit with the consciousness that we have developed during our lifetime. We then continue to grow spiritually within the world of spirit. So if I received advice at a reading from a loved one who left the physical plane with a very high state of consciousness, I would value an opinion from that person now in the world of spirit more than the advice of a spirit who, when alive, was always a total jerk.

Many people who receive readings seem to be under the impression that "because the advice comes from someone in the world of spirit, it is advice that should be followed." I do not agree.

Advice from a Medium

Who is in charge? You are, not the medium! Unfortunately there are some readers who take advantage of the opportunity to make money, and want clients to call them for advice often. However, a responsible medium will not tell her clients what to do, and readers who understand the true value of a mediumistic reading will not allow people to become overly dependent on them. In fact, many mediums will only see a client a few times a year, and some only once a year.

Rely on Your Common Sense

Ask yourself the following questions regarding the advice given:
- Is it common sense to follow this advice?
- Have I ever received this same advice before?
- Does following this advice seem like a positive thing to do?
- Is this good advice that I feel resistant to following?
- Does following the advice involve hard work that I am resistant to doing?

These are all good common-sense questions, and I am sure that you can add more to this list.

SHOULD YOU BELIEVE EVIDENCE YOU RECEIVE DURING A READING?

Evaluate what you heard in the reading. Was what you were told correct?

Unfamiliar Information

Were you given any evidence that you did not understand at the time? Hopefully you either have a tape recording of your reading or you have taken notes. Now you need to check out the pieces of information that you could not recognize during the reading.

I once had a reading with a medium who brought me the name of Katherine in my family. While I did not recognize that name *during* the reading, when I checked with living members of my family *after* the reading, I found out that there is a Katherine.

On another occasion, I gave a reading to a woman and told her that the communicating spirit was showing me the image of a ring with a red stone that belonged to her uncle in spirit named Ralph. My client had identified the communicating spirit as her grandmother, but did not recognize this information about Ralph and his ring. But weeks later she told me that she had talked to her mother, who said that she did have a brother named Ralph in spirit—and she then opened a drawer and pulled out a ring with a red stone that had belonged to him.

This is the best sort of evidence. Why? When I first began doing mediumistic readings, I would be crushed when I brought a piece of evidence that a client could not recognize. But now when that happens I am actually excited, as I know how meaningful it will be to my client if that information is confirmed by a member of the family.

As I've explained, some people feel that the information we get in mediumistic readings is really psychic, and not information being brought by loved ones in spirit. But when a readee does not recognize a piece of evidence, and another family member later confirms that evidence, it is impossible to say that the evidence is psychic. If it were, the medium would have had to "read the mind" of the person in the family who knows about the evidence—a person who was not present during the reading. In other words, if I had been working on a psychic level when I told my client about her uncle

Ralph's red ring, I couldn't have received the information from the readee, who didn't know about it. I would have had to receive it from the mind of the readee's mother, who *did* know the information, but who wasn't there! I find it much harder to believe that than to believe that I was communicating with the grandmother of the readee, who is now in spirit, and telling me about Uncle Ralph's red ring.

Others feel that when mediums get evidence, they are receiving it from some kind of "bank of information" that exists out in the cosmos. Personally, I find that also harder to believe than that I am communicating with spirits. I see, hear, and sense the spirits, and the spirits look and feel as if they are there. After doing many readings, I just know that the spirits are there. I don't feel as if I am getting information either from my client or from some incredible memory bank in the sky.

When You Don't Believe the Evidence

Sometimes you may believe the medium's evidence during the reading, but then afterward find it hard to believe what you heard. The reader may have brought you lots of excellent evidence, *or* you may just *think* that she did. That is why it is important that you either record a reading or take some notes. If you have written down that the medium said you have two sisters in spirit and that one of them is named Barbara, then you will not have to wonder after the reading whether you just imagined the medium told you that.

ASK YOURSELF WHY YOU DON'T BELIEVE IT

Are you an incurable skeptic? Think how many religions teach that there is an afterlife, and how many people believe that when we die there is some kind of existence beyond for the spirit. If so many of us believe that there are spirits existing in some kind of afterlife, why are we so surprised that these spirits can communicate with us?

If you are skeptical about the evidence you have received in your reading, accept that you are skeptical. If you cannot believe that your loved one was actually there communicating during your reading, even if you were brought really specific evidence, then just accept your feelings. Unless you have reason to believe that you are dealing with a dishonest medium, it is useless to spend hours wondering how the medium got that information.

Was the medium dishonest? Some people accuse all mediums of getting information prior to the reading, or somehow tricking the client into telling the information. *Yes, there are dishonest mediums, just as there are dishonest people in all lines of work.* Remember, a reputable medium will *not* try to get information from you, and will in fact want to know as little as possible about you before the reading so that the evidential quality of the information she brings will not be compromised. If a medium doesn't try to stop you from blurting out information, you may be in the wrong reading room!

Remember to get a personal recommendation before seeing a medium or watch the medium in a demonstration before making an appointment. Then, if you have been careful not to tell the medium anything about yourself or your loved ones prior to or during the reading, you have done your job well! If the medium brings you evidence about your loved ones in spirit, *with no prior knowledge of that evidence*, you can rest assured that you have had a good reading.

But most of us are honest and have come to be confident that we are truly communicating with those from the world of spirit.

Most of us are not interested in trying to convert you to our way of thinking. It took us years to reach the conclusion that we are talking with spirits. We are there to act as channels for those in the spirit world who want to communicate with you. As much as we are there to serve you, the readee, we are even more dedicated to serving those communicators in the world of spirit who are waiting for an opportunity to speak through someone like us, who can hear and see them. Our job is to bring you their messages. Then of course, your job is to evaluate what we bring.

As your coach, I advise you once again to avoid being a pushover without becoming so picky that you miss the credible evidence that is brought to you. Review chapter 6 about understanding the medium's evidence. You need to walk a fine line between credulity and skepticism, but then I have always felt that the best of life always exists on a fine line.

AFTERWORD

THE TOP BLEW OFF MY WORLD

Sometimes it is strange to be seeing people in two different dimensions. There was a time in my life, in fact most of my life, when I was only aware of the physical dimension. I wondered if there was an afterlife but did not really think so. I thought religions just made that up to make us all feel better.

In the past dozen years I have had a whole new dimension open up to me, and I no longer live in the same world I used to live in. Some people call the physical world and the spiritual world "two worlds." My experience is that we live in one world, but we only are aware of a tiny part of it. Well, for me the top has blown off the world I used to live in, and it has opened up into many dimensions I never knew existed.

This has been an exciting but hard journey for me, as I was not the type to believe that we can actually talk to people who have "died." I don't even use the word "died" anymore, as it seems like a term I can no longer relate to. When people are skeptical that we can communicate with spirits, I always say the same thing to them: "I don't blame you for being skeptical. If I had not had the experiences I have had in the last twelve years, I would not believe it either." I had to have many readings and see many demonstrations of mediumship before I became a believer.

I want to thank you for allowing me to be part of your journey. I have liked being your coach, and I hope you will open this book again whenever you need me. You may not believe it, but I really feel close to you—all of you out there who are interested in spirit communication. While I can't see you all, I can sense your presence. I guess after getting used to talking to spirits, feeling the presence of my readers is not such a hard stretch! All kidding aside, I know what a life-changing experience it can be to get a good reading from a medium. I want you to have that experience.

As your coach, allow me to remind you one last time that you will have this experience if you have the patience to attend a number of readings. I cannot tell you the exact number, as it depends on how quickly you are able to locate a medium who can give you the proof you need. And remember that the medium your friend thinks is incredible may not be the right medium for you. But the right medium is worth searching for and waiting for. Be open to every reading that you have. Don't be a pushover, but then don't be overly critical and picky either. Allow yourself to sense the presence of spirit. Know that over time you will receive the proof you need. You will hear from those loved ones you want to hear from. If you are fortunate, the very first time you have a reading, it will be the reading that changes your life forever.

Until we meet again.

RESOURCES

Here is a small list of resources with which I have had personal experience. This is by no means a complete list. You will find additional resources in both national and local New Age magazines and in the calendar sections of your local newspapers.

WEB SITES

Bob Olsen's Web sites
BestPsychicMediums.com
OfSpirit.com

Tony Santos's Web site
The Other Side
www.tonysantos.com

ORGANIZATIONS

American Federation of
Spiritualist Churches
145 Herring Pond Road
Buzzards Bay, MA 02532
USA
www.americanfederation.org

Arthur Findlay College
Stansted Hall
Stansted
Essex
CM24 8UD
UNITED KINGDOM
Phone: 01279 813636
www.arthurfindlaycollege.org

Edinburgh College of
Parapsychology
2 Melville Street
Edinburgh EH3 7NS
SCOTLAND
Phone: 0131 220 1433

International Spiritualist
Federation
Redwoods
Stansted Hall
Stansted Mountfitchet
Essex CM24 8UD
UNITED KINGDOM
www.isfederation.org

National Spiritualist Association
of Churches
General Offices
P.O. Box 217
Lily Dale, New York 14752
USA
Phone: 716 595-2000
www.nsac.org

TO CONTACT CAROLE LYNNE

Carole Lynne is a singer-songwriter and a vocal coach who teaches a spiritually oriented music practice called Singing for the Soul®. She is also a minister and certified medium with the American Federation of Spiritualist Churches. When she's not teaching music, she spends her time giving mediumship demonstrations and private readings throughout the United States and abroad. She is the author of *Heart and Sound: Discover Your Soul Voice*.

If you would like to make an appointment for a reading or learn more about spirit communication, write, call, or email Carole Lynne. Information on workshops, classes, and demonstrations in churches and meeting halls is also available.

Write:
Carole Lynne
Post Office Box 600183
Newton, MA 02460
USA
Call: 617-964-0058
Email: *CaroleLynne777@aol.com*
www.carolelynne.com

For information on Sing for the Soul® workshops and *Heart and Sound* visit: *www.singingforthesoul.com*